Police Actions

A Practical Guide

Richard Clayton
Hugh Tomlinson

with the assistance of

Andrew Davies
Georgina Middleton

JOHN WILEY & SONS
Chichester • New York • Weinheim • Brisbane
Singapore • Toronto

Copyright © 1997 by John Wiley & Sons Ltd,
Baffins Lane, Chichester,
West Sussex PO19 1UD, England

National   01243 779777
International   (+44) 1243 779777
e-mail (for orders and customer service enquiries): cs-books@wiley.co.uk
Visit our Home Page on http://www.wiley.co.uk
or http://www.wiley.com

Other Wiley Editorial Offices

John Wiley & Sons, Inc., 605 Third Avenue,
New York, NY 10158-0012, USA

WILEY-VCH Verlag GmbH, Pappelallee 3,
D-69469 Weinheim, Germany

Jacaranda Wiley Ltd, 33 Park Road, Milton,
Queensland 4064, Australia

John Wiley & Sons (Asia) Pte Ltd, 2 Clementi Loop #02-01,
Jin Xing Distripark, Singapore 129809

John Wiley & Sons (Canada) Ltd, 22 Worcester Road,
Rexdale, Ontario M9W 1L1, Canada

Library of Congress Cataloging-in-Publication Data

Clayton, Richard.
    Police actions : a practical guide / Richard Clayton, Hugh
Tomlinson.
        p.   cm.
    Includes index.
    ISBN 0-471-96865-X (pbk.)
        1. Tort liability of police—United States.   2. Police misconduct—
Law and legislation—United States.   3. Police—Complaints against—
United States.   I. Tomlinson, Hugh.   II. Title.
IN PROCESS
344.73'052—dc21   96–51971
                                                             CIP

British Library Cataloguing in Publication Data

A catalogue record for this book is available from the British Library

ISBN 0-471-96865-X

Typeset in 11/13pt Garamond by Dorwyn Ltd, Rowlands Castle, Hants
Printed and bound in Great Britain by Biddles Ltd, Guildford and King's Lynn
This book is printed on acid-free paper responsibly manufactured from sustainable forestation,
for which at least two trees are planted for each one used for paper production.

Contents

Preface

The past decade has seen a fundamental change in public attitudes towards the police. A number of widely publicised "miscarriage of justice" cases have focused public attention on the police misconduct in the conduct of criminal investigations. Despite the efforts of Chief Constables and the Police Complaints Authority, there remains a significant number of officers who are prepared to bend and break the rules in order to secure convictions. The victims of these rogue police officers have, increasingly, turned to the civil courts to obtain compensation.

When we first began to write about "civil actions against the police" 10 years ago, such actions were relatively rare and were unfamiliar to most general legal practitioners. The position has changed beyond recognition since the late 1980s. Civil actions against the police have become an important area of general litigation practice. It has become essential for solicitors who undertake criminal work to be able to deal with the civil claims against the police which arise from such actions. In some areas of the country such actions now come before the courts on a weekly basis. A very large percentage are settled before trial.

However, civil actions against the police present a number of serious practical difficulties for solicitors. In particular, they are the only area of civil work in the County Court which involves trial by jury. The post-1991 "automatic directions" regime does not apply. The Lord Chancellor's Department has found it necessary to issue special guidance on the conduct of police jury trials to new judges. This book attempts to provide such guidance for the general legal practitioner.

The relevant law is often difficult and archiac. We have attempted to summarise it in the first chapter. A comprehensive treatment of the law can be found in our book *Civil Actions against the Police* (Sweet and Maxwell, 3rd ed, 1998). The discussion of damages in the second chapter had to be completely revised at a late stage to take account of the path-breaking decision of the Court of Appeal in *Thompson* v *Commissioner of Police of the Metropolis* (now reported at [1997] 2 All ER 762) This case fixes, for the first time, "scales" of damages to be applied in actions for false imprisonment and malicious prosecution. The Court also gave detailed guidance on aggravated and exemplary damages. The *Thompson* case will introduce a welcome degree of certainty into the assessment of damages in police cases.

The largest part of the book is taken up with a detailed analysis of the procedural steps in a police action, from the taking of instructions to the conduct of a trial. The final chapter contains a full set of precedents. Our intention has been to provide a comprehensive and practical guide to all the procedural issues which arise in actions against the police.

We have been assisted in writing this book by Andrew Davies and Georgina Middleton of New Court Chambers who both have considerable practical experience in the area. We have also had the input and assistance of a number of other friends and colleagues including John Davis, Frederic Reynold QC, Alex Pelling and David Simon. Finally, we would like to thank our editor at John Wiley & Sons for her persistence in the face of the usual authorial delay. We have endeavoured to state the law as at 31 May 1997.

Richard Clayton

Devereux Chambers

Devereux Court

London WC2R 3JJ

Hugh Tomlinson

New Court Chambers

5 Verulam Buildings

Grays' Inn

London WC1R 5LY

19 June 1997

Tables

Table of Cases

Tables

Tables

Tables

Tables

Tables

Tables

Table of Rules of the Supreme Court

Table of County Court Rules

Table of Statutes

Tables

Contents of Chapter 1

Chapter 1
Basic Information

1. INTRODUCTION

When claims arise

Carrying out police duties necessarily involves serious interference with the legal rights of citizens. As an essential part of their duties the police:

- stop and search pedestrians or motorists;
- search premises and seize evidence;
- arrest and detain suspects;
- arrange the prosecution of suspected criminals.

Many of these activities would be, without further justification, illegal. But most of the time, the police do not break the law. They can justify otherwise unlawful acts by relying on their statutory or common law powers.

Nevertheless, these powers are limited and strictly construed. There are many situations in which the police act beyond their powers, either inadvertently (for example, a failure to comply with the rules governing detention) or deliberately (for example, an unprovoked assault by a police officer).

If the police cannot justify their acts by reference to their powers, the person affected can sue for damages. This book deals with the basic practice and procedure in such cases.

Whenever the police stop, search, arrest or detain someone, search their premises, seize their goods or unsuccessfully prosecute them, there is a potential civil action. In practice, the most common areas of complaint leading to civil actions are:

- the use of unprovoked or unreasonable force;
- searches of the person, including "strip searches";
- arrests which are unjustified due to lack of proper grounds or failure to give proper reasons;

- unjustifiably long periods of detention in police custody;
- prosecution on the basis of fabricated evidence or for improper motives.

There are other areas which may give rise to legal proceedings, such as police surveillance, misfeasance in a public office, negligence, or judicial review.

On close examination, a large proportion of criminal cases give rise to potential civil actions. Solicitors can obtain a preliminary view about which cases could lead to civil proceedings by including a short pro forma questionnaire in all criminal briefs asking counsel about the prospects of successfully suing the police. Even when the plaintiff is in fact convicted of a criminal offence, a civil action against the police may lie – for example, because of his treatment on arrest or in custody. All cases merit careful investigation, particularly as a civil action is, at present, the only effective remedy that a person has against police misconduct. In 1994, only 2.17% of complaints against the police were found to be substantiated[1] whereas nearly 50% of plaintiffs who brought civil proceedings against the police obtained compensation.

Police powers

There are three kinds of powers which the police can rely on to justify their actions:

(i) common law powers;
(ii) statutory "without warrant" powers;
(iii) statutory "with warrant" powers.

Common law powers are constantly being eroded by statute. Nevertheless, some important common law powers remain: for example, that of arrest or entry for breach of the peace, or seizing the "fruits, instruments or evidence" of serious crime. These powers are defined only by case law.

Statutory powers, both with and without warrant cover most areas of police activity. The majority of these are now found in the

---

[1]Home Office Statistical Bulletin 13/95, 28 June 1995.

Police and Criminal Evidence Act 1984 ("PACE"). Powers granted by statute are strictly construed:

> "if the statutory words relied upon as authorising the acts are ambiguous or obscure, a construction should be placed upon them that is least restrictive of individual rights which would otherwise enjoy the protection of common law".[2]

2. TRESPASS TO THE PERSON

There are three forms of trespass to the person. They are assault, battery and false imprisonment.

Assault and battery

Battery is the direct imposition of unlawful physical contact. An assault takes place when the plaintiff has cause to apprehend the immediate infliction of such contact.[3] Batteries cover the whole range of physical contact from severe beating to simple touching[4] and in order for an action to lie there is no need for the plaintiff to suffer physical injury or even pain. However, the physical contacts of ordinary life are not illegal, either because everyone gives implied consent to them, or because of a more general exception to the prohibition on non-consensual touching, based on the exigencies of everyday life. In such a case, the burden of proving absence of consent lies on the plaintiff[5] regardless of whether the allegation is that the plaintiff expressly rejected the contact, or that the contact exceeded the boundaries of generally accepted conduct. Thus, a "tapping on the shoulder" by a police officer may not be a battery[6] since it is for the tribunal of fact to decide whether the physical contact goes beyond what is acceptable by the ordinary standards of everyday life.[7]

---

[2]Per Lord Diplock, *R* v *IRC,* ex p *Rossminster* [1980] AC 952, 1008, HL; see also, *Morris* v *Beardmore* [1981] AC 446, 463.
[3]See *Clerk & Lindsell on Torts,* (17th ed, Sweet and Maxwell) para 583.
[4]*Collins* v *Wilcock* [1984] 1 WLR 1172.
[5]*Freeman* v *Home Office* [1984] 2 WLR 802, CA.
[6]*Donnelly* v *Jackman* [1970] 1 WLR 562, DC.
[7]*Mepstead* v *DPP* [1996] Crim LR 111.

Express, as well as implied, consent may provide a defence to an action in assault or battery. When the defendant maintains that the plaintiff consented to the force used against him, it is necessary to consider whether the consent covers the degree of force, or the type of force, which has been used. Furthermore, consent induced by pressure, fraud or abuse of authority may be null and void, so that an action will lie in battery.[8] In *Freeman* v *Home Office*[9] the judge accepted that an abuse of authority by the defendants could vitiate apparent consent without evidence of the use or threat of physical force.

The following acts have been held to be batteries:

- taking hold of a person's arm;[10]
- taking an object someone is holding;[11]
- taking someone's fingerprints.[12]

Reasonable force

The police will be justified in using "reasonable force" in the following situations:

- to prevent a breach of the peace which is being committed or which is reasonably apprehended;
- to prevent a crime or assist in the lawful arrest of offenders;[13]
- in the course of a lawful arrest;[14]
- if necessary, in the exercise of any power conferred by PACE.[15]

What is "reasonable" depends on all the circumstances. The force used must be "proportionate". A person who is assaulted by police officers in any of the above situations will be entitled to sue if excessive force is used.[16] Whether or not the force used is excessive must be judged on an objective basis.[17]

---

[8] *Bowater* v *Rowley Regis Corporation* [1944] KB 476.
[9] [1984] 2 WLR 802.
[10] *Kenlin* v *Gardner* [1967] 2 QB 510, DC.
[11] *Green* v *Goddard* (1704) 2 Salk 641.
[12] *Dumbell* v *Roberts* [1944] 1 All ER 326, 330.
[13] Criminal Law Act 1967, s 3.
[14] *Ibid.*
[15] PACE, s 117; see *Parry* v *Sharples* (17 July 1991, unreported) CA.
[16] *Allen* v *Commissioner of Metropolitan Police* [1980] Crim LR 441.
[17] See *Sturley* v *Commissioner, The Times* 27 June 1984, CA; *Rodriguez* v *Home Office* (1989) Legal Action, 14 February.

Basic Information

Plaintiff's behaviour

There is some disagreement over whether the way in which the plaintiff behaves can provide a further defence to an action for assault and battery. In *Murphy* v *Culhane*,[18] Lord Denning MR suggested that a man who takes part in a criminal affray may be said to have been guilty of such a wicked act as to deprive himself of a cause of action or alternatively, to have taken upon himself the risk. However, in *Revill* v *Newberry*,[19] the Court of Appeal rejected *ex turpi causa* as a defence in an action for negligence by a burglar shot by his victim.

Search of the person

Whenever the police search someone it will be a battery unless the search is justified by one of their powers. Any search will, therefore, be illegal unless the police can rely on one of the following:

- they have reasonable grounds to suspect that they will find stolen or prohibited articles;[20]
- the suspect has been arrested and there are reasonable grounds to believe that he is a danger to himself or others;[21]
- the suspect has been arrested and they are searching for evidence or anything which might be used to help him escape;[22]
- the suspect has been arrested and taken to a police station and the custody officer considers a search necessary to enable him to record everything the arrested person has with him.[23]

Even if a search is justified under these powers, it will be illegal if the reason for it is not given[24] or if it is made as a matter of course without considering the circumstances of the individual case.[25] If, however, there were in fact reasonable grounds for the search, it

---

[18] [1977] QB 94, CA.
[19] [1996] 2 WLR 239.
[20] PACE, s 1.
[21] PACE, s 32(1).
[22] PACE, s 32(2)(a).
[23] PACE, s 54(6).
[24] *Brazil* v *Chief Constable of Surrey* (1984) 148 JP 22.
[25] *Lindley* v *Rutter* [1981] 1 QB 128, DC.

may be lawful even if carried out as a matter of routine.[26] A routine search to establish a suspect's identity is unlawful.[27]

The recent amendments to Code C (Detention, Treatment and Questioning of Persons)[28] provide, for the first time, express restrictions on the procedure for strip searches.[29] Although it has been suggested that there is a new tort of "unlawfully inducing a person to remove his/her clothes",[30] it is submitted that an unlawful strip search should give rise to an action either in assault or false imprisonment, and that there is no need (or justification) for a new tort.

False imprisonment

The law attaches supreme importance to the liberty of the individual.[31] The tort of false imprisonment is one of the mechanisms whereby that liberty is protected by the law.

False imprisonment can be defined as complete deprivation of liberty for any time without lawful excuse. Although detaining someone will usually involve the use of force, it can be done by the assertion of legal authority[32] or even by dissuading someone from leaving confinement.[33]

In general, the police have no power to detain someone for questioning short of arrest.[34] A person who attends voluntarily at a police station without being arrested is, therefore, entitled to leave at will.[35] If the police pressurise him or her to stay they will be guilty of false imprisonment. They can rely on the following powers of detention:

- stop and search.[36]
- "drug search".[37]
- exercise of a power under PACE.

---

[26]*Middleweek* v *Chief Constable of Merseyside* [1992] 1 AC 179, CA.
[27]*R* v *Eeet* [1983] Crim LR 806.
[28]Code C, Annex A, Pt B.
[29]*ie*, "a search involving the removal of more than outer clothing".
[30]*Bayliss* v *Home Secretary* February 1993 Legal Action 16.
[31]See *Murray* v *Ministry of Defence* [1988] 1 WLR 629, HL.
[32]*Warner* v *Ruddiford* (1858) 4 CB (NS) 180.
[33]*Harnett* v *Bond* [1925] AC 669.
[34]*Kenlin* v *Gardner* [1967] 2 QB 510, DC.
[35]PACE, s 29; Code C, para 3.15.
[36]PACE, s 1.
[37]s 23(2) Misuse of Drugs Act 1971.

Basic Information

Arrest

The police have five types of power of arrest:

(i)   if they have reasonable grounds for suspecting that a person is committing, about to commit, or is guilty of an arrestable offence;[38]

(ii)   at common law, to prevent an actual or apprehended breach of the peace;

(iii) if they have reasonable grounds to suspect that a non-arrestable offence has been committed and one of the "general arrest conditions" is fulfilled;[39]

(iv)   under an arrest warrant;

(v)   under specific statutes, for example, Customs & Excise Acts, sections 12 and 25 of the Theft Act 1968.

The lawfulness of an arrest depends upon the existence of a power of arrest. If the police arrest someone but cannot show that they were relying on one of these powers, the arrest will be unlawful and they will be liable for false imprisonment. This is sometimes called "wrongful arrest" but there is no separate tort of this name. However, an otherwise lawful arrest will not be rendered unlawful by the use of undue force in the course of the arrest.[40]

The fact that a police officer believed that he had a power of arrest is not sufficient. He must actually have had the power.[41]

The reason for an arrest is now shown on a person's custody record. If the police subsequently attempt to justify the arrest on other grounds then this will provide good material for cross-examination.

Reasons for arrest

Even if an arresting officer is properly exercising a power of arrest, the arrest will be unlawful unless the person arrested is informed of the ground for the arrest at the time of, or as soon as is practicable

---

[38]PACE, s 24(4), (5), (6) and (7).

[39]PACE, s 25.

[40]*Simpson* v *Chief Constable of South Yorkshire Police, The Independent,* 27 February 1991, CA.

[41]*Wershof* v *Metropolitan Police Commissioner* [1978] 3 All ER 540.

after, the arrest.[42] This applies whether or not the ground for the arrest is obvious.[43] However, an arrest which is unlawful for failure to comply with section 28 will become lawful from the moment that proper information is given.[44]

The reasons for the arrest should be stated in sufficient detail for the suspect to be able to give a convincing denial.[45] For example, saying "you are under arrest for burglary" is not sufficient, the date and place of the alleged burglary should be specified.[46]

Arrest without warrant

The most common type of arrest is without warrant for an arrestable offence. When it is claimed that an arrest under this power is unlawful, there are four questions to be considered:

(i)   was the arrest for an arrestable offence?
(ii)   did the arresting officer in fact suspect that the person arrested was guilty of the offence? – the "subjective question";
(iii) was there reasonable cause for that suspicion? – the "objective question";
(iv)   was the officer's discretion to arrest exercised lawfully? – this is a "public law" question.

A number of common offences such as assaulting or obstructing the police are not arrestable and any arrest for them without warrant will be unlawful unless the "general arrest conditions" in section 25 of PACE are fulfilled or if the police can show that the arrest was, in fact, for breach of the peace.

It is usually straightforward for a police officer to establish that he had the relevant suspicion and exercised his discretion lawfully. But the question of "reasonable grounds" gives rise to considerable difficulties.

Reasonable cause will only be present if a reasonable man, in the position of the officer at the time of the arrest, would have thought

---

[42]PACE, s 28(3).
[43]PACE, s 28(4).
[44]*Lewis* v *Chief Constable of South Wales* [1991] 1 All ER 206, CA.
[45]*R* v *Telfer* [1976] Crim LR 562.
[46]*Murphy* v *Oxford* (15 February 1985, unreported), CA.

10

that the suspect was probably guilty of the offence.[47] This is a question of fact to be determined from all the circumstances, to be decided by the judge on the basis of the jury's findings of fact about what happened and what the officers believed.

Is there any duty to make inquiries?

There is some doubt as to what extent a police officer is under a duty to make inquiries before concluding that he has reasonable grounds to suspect that a person is guilty of an offence. There is authority that police officers should make all presently practicable enquiries before making an arrest.[48] In *Castorina* v *Chief Constable of Surrey*[49] the Court of Appeal suggested that the question of "further inquiries" is only relevant to whether or not a police officer with reasonable grounds to suspect is lawfully exercising his public law discretion to arrest. However, in *Mabey* v *The Chief Constable of Hampshire*[50] the Court of Appeal accepted that "the Judge was entitled to ask himself whether the contrary indications [which emerged prior to arrest] introduced such doubt into an objective consideration as rendered the suspicion which the officer initially had no longer reasonable".

A police officer can rely on hearsay evidence from a fellow officer.[51] It is arguable that when an officer relies on the appearance of a person on a "wanted" list he acts as a "mere conduit" and the person who must have reasonable grounds is the officer who put the name on the list.[52]

Breach of the peace

A breach of the peace must involve actual or threatened harm to person or property.[53] "Public alarm and excitement" or "being a

---

[47]See *Dallison* v *Caffrey* [1965] 1 QB 348, 371 and *O'Hara* v *Chief Constable of RUC* [1997] 2 WLR 1.
[48]*Dumbell* v *Roberts* [1944] 1 All ER 326, 329.
[49][1988] 138 NLJ 180, CA.
[50]29 June 1995, unreported, CA.
[51]*Moss* v *Jenkins* [1975] RTR 25, DC.
[52]See *Millington* v *Metropolitan Police Commissioner* 28 May 1983, unreported; but see *O'Hara op.cit.*
[53]*R* v *Howell* [1982] QB 416, CA.

nuisance and keeping one's neighbours awake" cannot of themselves constitute a breach of the peace.[54]

There is a common law power of arrest for wilfully obstructing the police in the execution of their duties where the nature of the obstruction is such that it actually causes, or is likely to cause, a breach of the peace.[55]

The general arrest conditions

Section 25 of PACE allows the police to arrest for any offence, however minor, provided that it appears to the officer that service of a summons is impractical and inappropriate because one of the "general arrest conditions" is satisfied.

The general arrest conditions are set out in section 25(3) of PACE. They are:

(i)   that the name of the relevant person is unknown to, and cannot be readily ascertained by, the constable;

(ii) that the constable has reasonable grounds for doubting whether a name furnished by the relevant person as his name is his real name;

(iii) that the relevant person has failed to furnish a satisfactory address for service, or the constable has reasonable grounds for doubting whether an address furnished by the relevant person is a satisfactory address for service;

(iv) that the constable has reasonable grounds for believing that an arrest is necessary to prevent the relevant person causing physical harm to himself or any other person, suffering physical injury, causing loss of or damage to property, committing an offence against public decency, or causing an unlawful obstruction of the highway;

(v)   that the constable has reasonable grounds for believing that arrest is necessary to protect a child or other vulnerable person from the relevant person.

---

[54] *Lewis* v *Chief Constable of Greater Manchester, The Times*, 22 October 1991. However, the violence (or threat of violence) need not emanate from the person arrested: it is enough if his or her conduct was such that violence from some third party was a natural consequence of his or her actions, as long as those actions were unreasonable. (*Percy* v *DPP* [1995] 1 WLR 1382, DC; *Nicol* v *DPP, The Times*, 22 November 1995.

[55] *Wershof* v *Metropolitan Police Commissioner* [1978] 3 All ER 540.

An address is a satisfactory address for service if it appears to the constable that the relevant person will be at it for a sufficiently long period for it to be possible to serve him with a summons, or that some other person specified by the relevant person will accept service of a summons for the relevant person at it.

Arrest with warrant

A warrant is a written authority which allows the police to do things which would otherwise be illegal. The police will not be liable for false imprisonment simply because the warrant was issued without jurisdiction.[56]

An arrest warrant may be executed anywhere in England and Wales by any person to whom it is directed or by any constable acting within his police area.[57] It can be executed notwithstanding that it is not in the constable's possession at the time but should be shown to the person arrested as soon as practicable.[58]

A police officer will be liable for false imprisonment when he arrests someone under a warrant in the following situations:

- if the person arrested is not the person named or described in the warrant;[59]
- if the arresting officer is not the person to whom the warrant is directed and is not within his police area;
- if the arresting officer does not give proper notice of the grounds of arrest;
- if the warrant has expired;
- if the arresting officer does not show the warrant to the person arrested as soon as practicable after the arrest.

Detention

A person arrested for an offence shall not be kept in police custody except in accordance with Part IV of PACE.[60] The provisions of Part

---

[56]Constables Protection Act 1750, s 6.
[57]Magistrates' Court Act 1980, s 125(2).
[58]*Ibid*, s 125(3).
[59]*Hoye* v *Bush* (1840) 1 Man & G 775.
[60]See s 34.

IV go beyond the common law position and, as such, should be strictly construed against the police.[61] However, Part IV does not apply to cases where, for instance, a person has been detained for a drug search[62] or arrested to prevent a breach of the peace.[63]

On arrival at the police station, a custody record is opened. The custody officer must decide whether there is sufficient evidence to charge the person arrested. If not, the person arrested must be released, either on bail or without bail, unless the custody officer has reasonable grounds for believing that his detention without being charged is *necessary*:

> "to secure or preserve evidence relating to an offence for which he is under arrest or to obtain such evidence by questioning him".[64]

Authorisation of detention for any other reason is unlawful and any subsequent detention will be a false imprisonment. Where detention is authorised for questioning in order to discover more details of the offence,

> "it is incumbent upon the custody officer to make sure that questioning for this purpose is not unduly postponed and to make sure that persons are not unnecessarily kept in custody".[65]

However, "necessary" has been given a broad construction by the Court of Appeal in *Wilding* v *Chief Constable*[66] in which Beldam LJ suggested that the question for the court was whether the custody sergeant's decision to detain was unreasonable in the sense that

> "no custody officer, acquainted with the ordinary use of language and applying his common sense to the competing considerations before him, could reasonably have reached that decision".

---

[61] *Hill* v *Chief Constable of South Yorkshire Police* [1990] 1 WLR 946, CA.
[62] s 23(2) Misuse of Drugs Act 1971.
[63] See *Marsh and White* v *Chief Constable of Hampshire*, (5 November 1992, unreported); *Joyce* v *Chief Constable of Hampshire* (29 September 1995, unreported).
[64] PACE, s 37(2).
[65] *Woods* v *Commissioner of Police for the Metropolis*, (26 May 1995, unreported), CA.
[66] 22 May 1995, unreported, CA.

Basic Information

In the first instance, a person may be detained without charge for up to 24 hours.[67] After six hours the detention must be "reviewed". The review officer must again decide whether there is sufficient evidence to charge the suspect.[68] Detention after the review can only be authorised on the same grounds as the original detention could have been authorised. The review officer must give the suspect or his solicitor an opportunity to make representations about the detention.[69]

A police officer of at least superintendent's rank can authorise detention for a further 12 hours.[70] This can only be done in the case of a "serious arrestable offence"[71] and if the investigation is being conducted "diligently and expeditiously".[72] Detention for a further period of up to 60 hours can be authorised by a magistrates' court.[73]

If any of the strict requirements of PACE are not complied with at any stage then the subsequent detention will be unlawful. The entries on the custody record should be checked very carefully against the statutory powers. This will often disclose breaches of the statutory provisions which make an initially lawful detention unlawful.

In summary, detention prior to charge will be unlawful in the following situations:

- if the custody officer fails to charge the suspect when there is sufficient evidence to do so;[74]
- if the custody officer authorises detention without the statutory grounds being satisfied;[75]
- if the custody officer charges the suspect but continues to detain him without the statutory grounds being satisfied;[76]
- if the custody officer becomes aware that the grounds for detention have ceased to apply but fails to release the suspect;[77]
- if the "reviews" are not conducted at all, or conducted improperly;

---

[67]PACE, s 41(1).
[68]PACE, s 40.
[69]PACE, s 40(12).
[70]PACE, s 42.
[71]Defined by PACE, s 116.
[72]PACE, s 42(1).
[73]PACE, s 43.
[74]See R v Holmes, ex p Sherman [1981] 2 All ER 612, DC.
[75]PACE, s 37(2).
[76]PACE, s 38(1).
[77]PACE, s 34(2).

- if the detention without charge continues beyond 24 hours without proper authorisation.

Where a person arrested for an offence is charged, the custody officer must authorise that person's release from police detention, either on bail or without bail, unless (in the case of an adult), one of the conditions in section 38(1)(a), as amended by the Criminal Justice and Public Order Act 1994, is satisfied. These are:

- that the arrested person's name and address cannot be ascertained or the custody officer has reasonable grounds for doubting whether a name or address furnished by him as his name and address is his real name or address;
- the custody officer has reasonable grounds for believing that the person arrested will fail to appear in court to answer bail;
- in the case of a person arrested for an imprisonable offence, the custody officer has reasonable grounds for believing that the detention of the person arrested is necessary to prevent him from committing an offence;
- in the case of a person arrested for an offence which is not an imprisonable offence, the custody officer has reasonable grounds for believing that the detention of the person arrested is necessary to prevent him from causing physical injury to any other person or from causing loss of or damage to property;
- the custody officer has reasonable grounds for believing that the detention of the person arrested is necessary to prevent him from interfering with the administration of justice or with the investigation of offences or a particular offence;
- the custody officer has reasonable grounds for believing that the detention of the person arrested is necessary for his own protection.

The custody officer is required to have regard to the same considerations as those which a court is required to have regard to in taking the corresponding decisions under paragraph 2 of Part I of Schedule 1 to the Bail Act 1976: namely, the nature and seriousness of the offence and the probable method of dealing with the offender for it; the character, antecedents, associations and community ties of the accused; his "record" for answering bail in the past, and the strength of the evidence against him.

3. MALICIOUS PROSECUTION

Elements of the tort

A person who has been prosecuted by police officers may have a cause of action for malicious prosecution. In order to succeed in such an action the plaintiff must prove that:

- there has been a prosecution which has caused him damage;
- the prosecution was instituted or continued by the police;
- the prosecution terminated in his favour;
- the prosecuting police officer acted without reasonable and probable cause;
- the prosecuting police officer acted maliciously.

Damage

This results when the plaintiff is charged with an imprisonable of-fence, if the charge was necessarily defamatory of the plaintiff or if the plaintiff has incurred any costs in defending the charge.[78] The only cases in which this element of the tort will produce difficulties is when the plaintiff was charged with very minor "technical" offences.

The prosecution

Although the conduct of prosecutions is now in the hands of the Crown Prosecution Service, an individual police officer will "in-stitute" proceedings if he makes a report implicating the plaintiff in a crime. The fact that the actual decision to prosecute is taken by someone else is irrelevant.[79]

Favourable termination

This has a wide sense and covers the following possibilities:

- an acquittal after a full trial;

---

[78] *Berry* v *British Transport Commission* [1962] 1 QB 306, CA.
[79] *Malz* v *Rosen* [1966] 1 WLR 1008.

- the prosecution being discontinued with the leave of the court;[80]
- the refusal by justices to commit at the end of committal proceedings;
- the indictment being quashed for formal reasons;[81]
- a conviction being quashed on appeal;[82]
- the prosecution offering no evidence after the defendant has agreed to be bound over.[83]

Proceedings after conviction

Although a conviction is obviously not a favourable termination there are two common situations in which it may be possible to bring a malicious prosecution action after conviction:

(i)   where the plaintiff was acquitted as charged but convicted of a less serious offence;[84]

(ii) where the plaintiff charged with a number of offences was only convicted on some counts. There will then be a favourable termination in relation to the counts on which he was acquitted.[85]

Lack of reasonable and probable cause

The plaintiff must prove a negative – that the police officer did not have reasonable and probable cause for belief in his guilt. In many cases there is a simple conflict of fact between the plaintiff and police officers: the plaintiff's version is that he did nothing wrong; according to the police the plaintiff committed an offence. In such cases, the proof of lack of reasonable and probable cause is simple – if the jury accept the plaintiff's version of events it follows that the police did not have proper grounds to prosecute him and therefore lacked reasonable and probable cause.

---

[80] *Watkins* v *Lee* (1839) 5 M&W 270.
[81] *Wicks* v *Fentham* (1791) 4 Term Rep 247.
[82] *Herniman* v *Smith* [1938] AC 305.
[83] *Hourihane* v *Metropolitan Police Commissioner*, *The Times*, 27 December, 1994.
[84] *Boaler* v *Holder* (1887) 3 TLR 546.
[85] *Leibo* v *Buckman* [1952] 2 All ER 1057, CA.

Basic Information

In more complex cases, the issue of reasonable and probable cause can be divided into four questions:

- did the prosecutor have an honest belief in the guilt of the accused?
- did the prosecutor have an honest conviction of the existence of the facts relied on?
- was this conviction based on reasonable grounds?
- did the matters relied on constitute reasonable and probable cause for the belief in the accused's guilt?

The first two questions are for the jury who should be asked "Did the defendant honestly believe in the charges he was making?"[86] If the answer to this question is "no" then the prosecutor lacks reasonable and probable cause. The prosecutor need not believe that the accused was guilty[87] but only that there is a prima facie case.[88]

The third and fourth questions are for the judge – on the basis of facts found by the jury. There will be no reasonable and probable cause if the circumstances before the prosecutor would not have led an ordinarily prudent and cautious person to conclude that the accused was probably guilty of the offence.[89] Such a person would take proper steps to inform himself of the true state of the case,[90] consider the matter on admissible evidence only[91] and, in all but the simplest cases, put the facts before experienced counsel and receive advice that the prosecution is justified.[92]

The fact that a person was committed for trial or convicted by a court of first instance does not seem to be decisive of the question of reasonable and probable cause. Lack of reasonable and probable cause can never be inferred from malice.[93]

The proof of lack of reasonable and probable cause can be approached by three routes. First, if only one version of events is correct and the plaintiff's version is accepted he is entitled to succeed. Secondly, the plaintiff will also succeed if he can show that

---

[86] *Dallison* v *Caffrey* [1965] 1 QB 348, CA.
[87] *Tempest* v *Snowden* [1952] 1 KB 130, CA.
[88] *Glinski* v *McIver* [1962] AC 726, 766–7.
[89] *Ibid.*
[90] *Abrath* v *North East Railway Co* [1883] 1 QBD 440; *Phillips* v *Naylor* (1859) 4 H&N 565.
[91] *Meering* v *Grahame-White Aviation* (1919) 122 LT 44.
[92] *Abbott* v *Refuge Assurance Co* [1962] 1 QB 432, 454–5, CA.
[93] *Glinski* v *McIver* [1962] AC 726, CA.

the police officers did not in fact believe that he had committed the offence – because, for example, they had fabricated a confession or planted evidence. Thirdly, the plaintiff can try to show that, however honest the prosecutor was, a reasonable person would not have brought a prosecution in those circumstances. The difficulty with this route is that it is likely to be difficult to prove that an honest but incompetent prosecutor was also malicious. There is no tort of "negligent prosecution" and no action will lie if the police mistakenly prosecute someone, however incompetent they have been, if malice cannot be proved.[94]

Malice

This does not mean spite or hatred but simply "wrongful motive".[95] It is malicious to prosecute someone to deter others[96] or because he has given evidence against the police in previous proceedings.[97]
There are three ways to establish malice:

(i)   by establishing some specific improper motive on the part of the police officers;
(ii) by establishing that the police have fabricated evidence or lied about the circumstances of the offence;[98]
(iii) by inference from the absence of reasonable and probable cause.

Malicious process

An action in malicious prosecution cannot be brought in respect of proceedings which cannot possibly have a "favourable termination" – for example, the procurement of a warrant. Nevertheless, an action in tort will lie for the malicious use of legal proceedings, falling short of prosecution. The plaintiff must prove that the police officer

(i)   maliciously

---

[94]See *Kumar* v *Metropolitan Police Commissioner*, (31 January 1995, unreported), CA.
[95]*Mitchell* v *Jenkins* (1833) 5 B & Ad 588, 595.
[96]*Stevens* v *Midland Railway Company* (1854) 10 Ex 353, 356.
[97]*Glinski* v *McIver* [1962] AC 726, CA.
[98]See *White* v *Metropolitan Police Commmissioner*, *The Times*, 24 April 1982.

(ii)   instituted some legal process
(iii) without reasonable and probable cause
(iv)   which caused him damage.

Thus, it is an actionable wrong to procure the issue of a search warrant, without reasonable or probable cause and maliciously.[99] There is a tort of "malicious arrest", for example, for failure to answer a witness summons.[100] It is also actionable to lay an information to have someone bound over to keep the peace under section 115 of the Magistrates Court Act 1980 – provided that the person is not in fact bound over.[101] The plaintiff must establish some specific financial damage arising out of the application to bind over. An action for malicious process will lie if the police maliciously and without reasonable and probable cause apply for a warrant of further detention under section 43 of PACE.

4. WRONGFUL SEARCH AND SEIZURE

Trespass to land

Any unjustified direct physical intrusion onto land in possession of another is a trespass. The slightest entry is sufficient – for example, putting a foot in the door. Honest belief in a right to enter is not a defence.[102]

Any person is entitled to enter premises if the occupier gives him express permission or licence to enter. This permission may be given by a member of the occupier's family[103] or his guests.[104] Anyone who has a genuine reason to enter a house has an implied licence to approach the front door through the garden.[105]

An express or implied licence can be revoked at any time by the occupier. Express words of revocation must be used so, for example, "fuck off" will not be enough.[106]

---

[99] Reynolds v Commissioner of Police of the Metropolis [1985] QB 881, 886, HL.
[100] Roy v Prior [1971] AC 470, HL.
[101] Everett v Ribbands [1952] 2 QB 198.
[102] Hewlitt v Bickerton (1947) 150 EG 421.
[103] Faulkner v Willetts [1982] RTR 159.
[104] Jones & Jones v Lloyd [1981] Crim LR 340, DC.
[105] Brunner v Williams (1975) 73 LGR 266, DC.
[106] Snook v Mannion [1982] Crim LR 601, DC.

Once a licence has been revoked, the person who has entered under it has a reasonable time to leave. He then becomes a trespasser and reasonable force may then be used to eject him.[107] A police officer who enters under an authority given by law becomes a trespasser *ab initio* if he abuses that authority.[108]

Justifications for entry

The police may enter premises under the authority of a search warrant. There is a common law power of entry "to deal with or prevent a breach of the peace" (PACE, section 17(6)). They can enter to deal with breaches of the peace which are actually in progress or apprehended.[109] They can also enter in the fresh pursuit of someone suspected of a breach of the peace which has occurred elsewhere. However, when the pursuit ends and there is no likelihood of it recurring, there is no common law power to enter.[110]

In addition, the police have seven statutory powers of entry:

(i)   to execute an arrest warrant;[111]

(ii)   to arrest for an arrestable offence;[112]

(iii) to arrest for certain specified offences;[113]

(iv)   to recapture a person unlawfully at large;[114]

(v)   to save life, limb or property;[115]

(vi)   to search the premises of a person under arrest for evidence;[116]

(vii) to search premises where a person was arrested or in which he was immediately before he was arrested.[117]

---

[107]See *Davis* v *Lisle* [1936] 2 KB 434.
[108]*Six Carpenters Case* (1610) 8 Co Rep 146a.
[109]*McLeod* v *Metropolitan Police Commissioner* [1994] 4 All ER 553, CA.
[110]*R* v *Marsden* (1868) LR 1 CCR 131.
[111]PACE, s 17(1)(a).
[112]PACE, s 17(1)(b).
[113]PACE, s 17(1)(c).
[114]PACE, s 17(1)(d).
[115]PACE, s 17(1)(e).
[116]PACE, s 18(1).
[117]PACE, s 32(2)(b).

The first four powers are only exercisable if the constable has reasonable grounds to believe that the person sought is on the premises.[118] The seventh (section 32) power requires reasonable grounds for believing that there is evidence for which a search is permitted under that paragraph on the premises. This means evidence relating to the offence for which the arrest was made.

Interference with goods

There are two torts relating to interference with goods: trespass to goods and conversion. Any unjustified direct physical interference with goods in a person's possession is a *trespass to goods*. Any direct physical interference will be sufficient.[119] If the police interfere with goods, without lawful justification, in a manner inconsistent with the rights of the person in possession, they will be guilty of *conversion*.

Proceedings can be brought for trespass to goods when goods are removed, damaged or even touched by the police. Conversion will be more appropriate if the plaintiff is prevented from gaining access to his goods, if lawfully seized goods are lost or damaged or if they refuse to return goods which are no longer needed for the purpose for which they were seized.

Justifications for seizure of goods

The police have a common law power to seize the "fruits", "evidence" or "instruments" of serious crime from anyone "implicated" in the crime or who unreasonably refuses to hand them over.[120] These powers have been superseded (but not replaced) by powers under PACE.

The police have powers to enter premises and seize goods under a wide range of statutes. PACE provides for seven powers of seizure without warrant. The police may seize

---

[118] PACE, s 17(2)(a).
[119] *Fouldes* v *Willoughby* (1841) 8 M & W 540, 549.
[120] *Ghani* v *Jones* [1970] 1 QB 693, 708–9, CA.

23

(i)   items obtained through crime which may be disposed of;[121]

(ii)   evidence of crime which may be disposed of;[122]

(iii) information on a computer which may be disposed of;[123]

(iv) evidence found on the premises of a person under arrest;[124]

(v)   evidence found on a stop and search;[125]

(vi) evidence found after arrest;[126]

(vii) property a person has with him when brought to a police station.[127]

When the police seize large quantities of goods they must consider each item separately and decide whether or not there are reasonable grounds for believing that it is seizable. If proper consideration is not given to each item, there will be a trespass to goods.[128]

Retention, access and copying

Although goods have been lawfully seized, the police will be guilty of wrongful interference with goods if they cannot justify their continuing retention. When the police seize an item under their common law powers they must not keep it for longer than is reasonably necessary for their investigations.[129] The property must be returned when charges are dropped or the proceedings have been disposed of.

The common law position is confirmed by PACE, section 22, under which any material seized may be retained for "so long as is necessary in all the circumstances". Goods may be retained if there are reasonable grounds for believing they are the fruits of crime.[130] If goods are seized from a person in custody on the ground that they might be used to cause injury, damage property, interfere with evidence or assist in escape, they must be returned when the person is released from custody.[131] No goods can be retained for use

---

[121]PACE, s 19(2).
[122]PACE, s 19(3).
[123]PACE, s 19(4).
[124]PACE, s 18(1).
[125]PACE, s 1(6).
[126]PACE, s 32(2)(a).
[127]PACE, s 54(1) & (3).
[128]*Reynolds* v *Commissioner of Police of the Metropolis* [1985] QB 881, CA.
[129]*Ghani* v *Jones* [1970] 1 QB 693, CA.
[130]PACE, s 22(2)(b).
[131]PACE, s 22(3).

as evidence at a trial or for investigation if a photograph or a copy would be sufficient.[132]

The owner of documents has rights of access and copying under section 21 of PACE. There is a right to access to something retained for the purpose of investigating an offence unless the police have reasonable grounds for believing that to give access would prejudice the investigation.[133]

In summary, the owner of goods seized by the police will be able to sue for wrongful interference with goods in the following situations:

- if the police retain the goods longer than is "reasonably necessary";
- if the goods are not returned when the proceedings have finished;
- if the goods were seized because they might cause injury and they are not returned after the person is released;
- if a copy would have been sufficient for police purposes.

Search warrants

A number of statutes empower justices of the peace to issue search warrants. The procedure for applying for such warrants is laid down by PACE. When a search is conducted under a warrant an action for trespass to land will lie if:

- the provisions relating to applications for search warrants are not complied with;[134]
- the provisions relating to the execution of search warrants are not complied with[135] – in particular if a "generalised search" is conducted under a warrant which only authorises searches for specific items;
- the searching officers do not have the warrant with them at the time of the search;

---

[132]PACE, s 22(4).
[133]PACE, s 21(8).
[134]PACE, s 15.
[135]PACE, s 16.

- the searching officers execute the warrant on the wrong premises.

Any unlawful act committed in the course of a search under a warrant may render the officers trespassers *ab initio.*

The safeguards imposed by sections 15 and 16 are "stringent in effect".[136] Searches have been held to be unlawful where:

- copies of the schedules to the warrants were not supplied to the applicant at the time of the search;[137]
- the enactment under which the warrant was issued was not specified.[138]

5. OTHER CAUSES OF ACTION

Misfeasance in public office

Police constables are holders of a public office.[139] As a result, they are liable for misfeasance in that office if they cause damage by acts or omissions which are a "malicious abuse" of that office. There are circumstances in which an action in misfeasance will be the only cause of action available. Take, for example, a case in which a police officer carries out a search under a search warrant which has been obtained lawfully but with a malicious motive. The search warrant would be a complete defence to an action for trespass but in this case the plaintiff would still be entitled to sue in misfeasance.

An action in misfeasance will also be available if police officers give someone orders which they know they have no power to give. If the person obeys the orders and suffers loss as a result there will be an action in misfeasance. An action may also lie if a police officer improperly provides information about previous convictions.[139a]

---

[136]*R* v *Central Criminal Court and British Railways Board, ex p AJD Holdings* [1992] Crim LR 669, DC.

[137]*R* v *Chief Constable of Lancashire, ex p Parker and McGrath* [1993] QB 577, DC.

[138]*R* v *Reading JJ, ex p South West Meats* (1992) 4 Admin LR 401, DC.

[139]*Lewis* v *Cattle* [1938] 2 KB 454, 457. The tort of misfeasance in public office consists of two alternative limbs. Under limb one, injury had either to be intended by a public officer to a plaintiff or to a class of persons to which the plaintiff belonged. Under limb two, the officer had to know that he had no power to do the act concerned and that the plaintiff or another class member would probably suffer loss as a result. For the purposes of the second limb, liability could arise due to actual knowledge of the *ultra vires* nature of the act concerned, or where the officer was reckless in ascertaining the truth of the position. See *Three Rivers District Council* v *Bank of England* [1996] 3 ALL ER 558.

[139a]See *Elliott* v *Chief Constable of Wiltshire, The Times,* 5 December 1996.

However, a person whose conviction for a crime is subsequently quashed cannot bring a civil action for conspiracy to pervert the course of justice or misfeasance in public office against police officers investigating the crime who, he alleged, had created a false record of an incriminating interview with him. The officers are protected by the rule of absolute immunity conferred as a matter of public policy in relation to witnesses, extending to conduct and statements prior to the commencement of proceedings if part of the investigation or of the preparation of the evidence.[140]

Negligence

The police, like all public authorities, can be sued in negligence if they are in breach of a duty of care. It is clear that a common law duty of care may arise in the performance of statutory functions. However, there is a broad distinction between (a) cases in which it is alleged that the authority owes a duty of care in the manner in which it exercises a statutory discretion, and (b) cases in which a duty of care is alleged to arise from the manner in which the statutory duty has been implemented in practice.[141]

If the plaintiff's complaint alleges carelessness, not in the taking of a discretionary decision to do some act, but in the practical manner in which that act has been performed, for example the conduct of a police investigation, the question whether or not there is a common law duty of care falls to be decided by applying ordinary principles, that is:

- Was the damage to the plaintiff reasonably foreseeable?
- Was the relationship between the plaintiff and the defendant sufficiently proximate?
- Is it just and reasonable to impose a duty of care?

Negligent acts

In many cases police negligence liability is clear and no special considerations need apply. For example, the police can be sued for

---

[140] *Silcott* v *Commissioner of Police for the Metropolis, The Times,* 9 July1996.
[141] See the speech of Lord Browne-Wilkinson in *X (Minors)* v *Bedfordshire County Council* [1995] 2 AC 633, HL, at 170–3.

negligent driving[142] even where they are in hot pursuit of suspects.[143] They owe a duty of care in directing traffic[144] and to people held in custody.[145]

In recent years the police have been successfully sued for negligence in the following cases:

- by the owner of a gun shop which was destroyed by fire after the police negligently failed to take proper fire precautions during a siege;[146]
- by the owner of a stolen car which was negligently returned to a thief;[147]
- by the widow of a man who was negligently left by the roadside whilst drunk on a winter night;[148]
- by the widow of a man who committed suicide in prison, the police having failed to inform the prison authorities that he was suicidal.[149]

Negligent investigations

It is often foreseeable that negligent police investigations will lead to damage. For example, if the police negligently fail to apprehend a criminal, then it may be foreseeable that he will have future victims. Nevertheless, it has been held that in the absence of special characteristics over and above simple foreseeability, the police do not owe a duty of care to individual members of the public to identify and apprehend an unknown criminal.[150] Furthermore, even if such a duty did exist public policy required that the police should not be liable. In *Alexandrou* v *Oxford*[151] the Court of Appeal held that an occupier of property connected by a burglar

---

142 *Wood* v *Richards* [1977] RTR 201, DC.
143 *Marshall* v *Osmond* [1983] QB 1034, CA.
144 *Knightley* v *Johns* [1982] 1 WLR 349, CA.
145 *Bryson* v *Northumbria Police Authority* [1977] CLY 2042.
146 *Rigby* v *Chief Constable of Northampton* [1985] 1 WLR 1242.
147 *Wilson (Charles)* v *Chief Constable of Greater Manchester* (18 January 1986, unreported) Manchester County Court.
148 *Allan* v *Chief Constable of Lothian & Borders* [1989] SLT 97.
149 *Kirkham* v *Anderton* [1990] 2 QB 283.
150 *Hill* v *Chief Constable of West Yorkshire* [1989] AC 53, HL.
151 [1993] 4 All ER 328, CA.

alarm to a police station does not stand in a special relationship to the police and there is, therefore, no duty of care owed to him by the police. Although a burglar was allowed to escape as a result of police carelessness, no damages could be recovered. In *Osman* v *Metropolitan Police Commissioner*[152] the Court of Appeal held that, prima facie, where the police had been informed on numerous occasions that an identified individual had threatened to harm a particular person, a duty of care could arise. However, the court went on to hold that public policy prevented the imposition of such a duty on the police as it would create a detrimentally defensive frame of mind towards policing. The police have no duty of care to protect road users from hazards discovered by them whilst going about their duties.[153]

In *Swinney* v *Chief Constable of Northumbria*[154] the Chief Constable appealed against the refusal to strike out a claim for damages for personal injuries suffered as a result of police officers' failure to keep secure confidential information supplied by the plaintiff concerning the death of an officer. The document was stolen and fell into the hands of the suspect, who threatened the plaintiff with violence and arson, resulting in psychological damage and financial loss. The appeal was dismissed on the basis that sufficient proximity existed between the parties, as the text of the document, and the repeated references to keeping the plaintiff's identity confidential highlighted the fact that he was distinguishable from the general public, and particularly at risk. The general immunity might not apply where other considerations of public policy (namely the need to protect informants) were important.

Negligent prosecutions

A defendant in criminal proceedings has no remedy in damages against the Crown Prosecution Service, in the absence of malice, arising out of the conduct of a prosecution against him.[155] The reasoning in *Elguzouli-Daf*, where the Commissioner did not apply

---

[152][1993] 4 ALL ER 344.
[153]*Ancell & Ancell* v *McDermott* [1993] 4 All ER 355, CA.
[154][1996] 3 WLR 968.
[155]*Elguzouli-Daf* v *Commissioner of Police of the Metropolis* [1995] QB 335, CA.

to strike out the claim against him, was extended to the police in *Kumar* v *Metropolitan Police Commissioner.*[156]

6. BREACHES OF THE CODES OF PRACTICE

The exercise by police of some of their powers under PACE is governed by Codes of Practice made under sections 60 and 66 of PACE. Code A deals with the exercise of statutory powers of stop and search. Code B covers the search of premises and the seizure of property. Code C deals with the detention, treatment and questioning of persons by police officers. Code D covers the identification of persons by police officers.

The breach of any provision of a Code of Practice does not give rise to any civil liability on the police.[157] Nevertheless, the codes are admissible in evidence in civil proceedings and they can be taken into account if the court considers them to be relevant.[158]

Breaches of the codes are only relevant when suing the police as:

- evidence of the lack of good faith on the part of the police – for example, failure to give reasons before a stop and search[159]
- aggravating factors in relation to the assessment of damages – for example the failure to provide blankets[160] or food[161] to a person in detention.

7. JUDICIAL REVIEW

The activities of chief officers of police and police authorities are subject to the supervision of the High Court under the judicial review procedure. The procedure may also be used to review the lawfulness of decisions by individual officers, such as the custody officer.[162]

---

[156]31 January 1995, unreported, CA.
[157]PACE, s 67(10).
[158]PACE, s 67(11).
[159]Code A, para 2.4.
[160]Code 8.3.
[161]Code C, para 8.6.
[162]R v *Chief Constable of Cambridgeshire, ex p Michel* [1991] 2 QB 499, DC.

Decision and sufficient interest

An applicant for judicial review must establish:

- "a sufficient interest in the matter to which the application relates";[163]
- that there has been a decision or justiciable issue susceptible of judicial review. In *R v Secretary of State for Employment, ex parte Equal Opportunities Commission*[164] the House of Lords held that the courts had jurisdiction to grant a declaration in the absence of a reviewable decision, because there was a properly justiciable issue.

Grounds for review

The grounds upon which the court will grant relief are limited. In *Council for Civil Service Unions* v *Minister for Civil Service.*[165] Lord Diplock defined the three main grounds as follows:

(i)   illegality
(ii)   irrationality[166]
(iii) procedural impropriety[167]

This classification is, however, not exhaustive.[168]

Examples

The courts are most reluctant to intervene in areas of police policy, particularly where the powers or duties in question are broadly expressed, such as the general duty to enforce the law.[169]

---

[163]Supreme Court Act 1981, s 31(3); RSC Ord 53 r3(1) and (7).

[164][1995] 1 AC 1, HL.

[165][1985] AC 374 at 410–411, HL.

[166]or "*Wednesbury* unreasonableness" after the case of *Associated Provincial Picture Houses* v *Wednesbury Corporation* [1948] 1 KB 223, CA.

[167]*i.e.*, breach of the rules of natural justice.

[168]See *R v Hillingdon LBC ex p Pulhofer* [1986] AC 484.

[169]*R v Commissioner of Police of the Metropolis, ex p Blackburn* [1968] 2 QB 118, CA; *R v Commissioner of Police of the Metropolis, ex p Blackburn (No 3)* [1973] QB 241, CA.

The courts have been more prepared to intervene where the powers or duties in question are more specific, or where there has been a breach of Home Office guidelines.[170]

Procedure and remedies

The procedure for judicial review is set out in RSC Order 53. There are a number of important points:

- the application is dealt with in two stages: the leave stage, which is usually *ex parte* and may be dealt with on the papers alone, and the application itself;
- the application for leave must be brought promptly and, at the very latest, within three months of the date when the grounds for the application first arose, unless there are good reasons for extending the time limit;
- an applicant may now seek one of the traditional prerogative orders (certiorari, mandamus, and prohibition), and declarations, injunctions, and damages.

8. BREACH OF CONFIDENCE

A duty of confidence arises when confidential information comes to the knowledge of a person in circumstances where he has notice, or is held to have agreed, that the information is confidential, with the effect that it would be just in all the circumstances that he should be precluded from disclosing the information to others. There are three limitations on the duty:[171]

(1) it only applies to information to the extent that it is confidential, and not already in the public domain;
(2) it does not apply to useless information or to trivia;
(3) the public interest that confidence should be preserved may be outweighed by some other countervailing public interest which favours disclosure.

---

[170]*R* v *Commissioner of Police for the Metropolis ex p P* (1996) 8 Admin LR 6 – decision to caution at police station; *R* v *Chief Constable of Kent ex p L* [1993] 1 All ER 756, DC – decision to prosecute rather than caution.
[171]See *Att-Gen* v *Guardian Newspapers (No 2)* [1990] 1 AC 109, HL.

Basic Information

In *Marcel* v *Commissioner of Police for the Metropolis*,[172] the Court of Appeal accepted that, subject to any express statutory provision, the police are authorised to seize, retain and use documents only for public purposes related to the investigation and prosecution of crime and the return of stolen property to the true owner. In *Hellewell* v *Chief Constable of Derbyshire*[173] Laws J agreed that a duty of confidence could arise when the police took a photograph of a suspect at a police station without his consent, but also held that, where the photograph was used reasonably for the prevention and detection of crime, the investigation of alleged offences, or the apprehension of suspects, the police would have a public interest defence to any action for breach of confidence. However, information as to previous convictions could not be confidential. These had been announced in open court and were in the public domain.[174]

[172][1992] Ch 225, CA.
[173][1995] 1 WLR 804.
[174]*Elliott* v *Chief Constable of Wiltshire*, *The Times*, 5 December 1996.

Contents of Chapter 2

Chapter 2
Damages and Other Remedies

1. DAMAGES IN GENERAL

If someone successfully sues the police, he will normally recover damages. Compensation will cover financial loss, physical injuries or injuries to feelings or reputation. The plaintiff is entitled to the amount of money which will, so far as money can do, put him into the same position he would have been in had the police misconduct never occurred.

However, this basic right to compensation is restricted by a number of general policy considerations. The most important of these are:

- remoteness;
- mitigation;
- contributory negligence.

Remoteness

Where damages are sought as a consequence of the defendant's negligence or breach of statutory duty, the plaintiff is entitled to any damages which result provided they are *reasonably foreseeable.*[1] Consequently, even if the plaintiff is unusually sensitive, the damages suffered will not be too remote provided that damages of that type could have been reasonably foreseen[2] for example, the fact that he has an unusually weak heart does not allow a defendant who acted negligently to say that the plaintiff cannot recover damages because he would have been less seriously injured if his heart had been normal.

---

[1] *Overseas Tankship (UK)* v *Morts Dock & Engineering (The Wagon Mound)* [1961] AC 388, PC.
[2] *Dulieu* v *White* [1901] 2 KB 669, 679.

On the other hand, where damages are sought for battery, false imprisonment, trespass to land or malicious prosecution, the plaintiff may well be entitled to damages for all direct consequences of the wrong, whether they are foreseeable or not.[3] For example, if the plaintiff is held in custody and misses a holiday he booked, he would be entitled to recover damages to compensate him for the holiday even though the damage was not reasonably foreseeable.

Mitigation

A plaintiff is under a duty to mitigate his damage by taking reasonable steps to minimise the losses caused to him by the defendant's wrong. Therefore, if he claimed compensation for losing his job as a result of a wrongful arrest, he would only recover damages for lost earnings for a period of time up to the point when it would become reasonable for him to have found new employment. If he claimed compensation for loss of earnings as a result of an assault and battery, duty to mitigate the loss may also require him to take up a different type of employment where, for example, he is no longer able to perform his original job due to the personal injuries sustained.

Contributory negligence

Even if the police have acted unlawfully, they can argue that a plaintiff's damages should be reduced if the plaintiff is guilty of contributory negligence[4] (except if they are liable for conversion or trespass to goods.[5] In practice, this will seldom arise because the police will have to show that the plaintiff acted unlawfully himself by, for example, assaulting the officer whom he accuses of battery.[6]

---

[3]See *Wilson* v *Pringle* [1987] QB 237 at 247, CA.
[4]See Law Reform (Contributory Negligence) Act 1945 s 1(1).
[5]Torts (Interference with Goods) Act 1977, s 11(1).
[6]See *Murphy* v *Culhane* [1977] QB 94, CA.

2. **COMPENSATORY DAMAGES**

Introduction

A plaintiff is entitled to "basic"[7] or compensatory damages to compensate him both for the financial losses he can quantify and the non-financial damage which the court will put a figure on. The plaintiff's quantifiable losses up to the date of trial are "special damages". All other damages including future loss of earnings are "general damages".

Special damages

The special damages which are potentially recoverable will obviously vary from case to case. The typical situations in which a plaintiff will recover special damages include:

- damage to clothing from an assault;
- the cost of any medical expenses incurred;
- lost earnings from time off work;
- the cost of repairing or replacing property damaged by the police;
- legal costs incurred by the plaintiff in defending himself if he succeeds in malicious prosecution.

General damages

Awards of general damages will be made, for example, for the distress and anxiety experienced during a period of false imprisonment, and the loss of future earnings arising due to injuries suffered by a plaintiff as a result of an assault. However, the way this is approached partly depends upon whether the case is tried by a judge and jury or a judge alone.

The pain and suffering a plaintiff sustains because of police misconduct justifies an award for just and reasonable damages and can include compensation for:

- the physical injuries and mental distress from being assaulted;

---

[7]See *Thompson* v *Commissioner of Police of the Metropolis* [1997] 2 All ER 774.

- the mental shock from suffering mistreatment at the hands of the police;
- the mental distress from experiencing being put in prison or serving a term of imprisonment when the police have acted unlawfully;
- the mental distress from fighting a false criminal prosecution;
- the mental distress caused by facing a potential prison sentence whilst fighting a false criminal prosecution;
- the mental distress caused by a potential or actual loss of livelihood which would result from a criminal conviction or prison sentence.

In false imprisonment cases a plaintiff is entitled to compensation for the loss of his liberty; this may overlap with the mental distress he feels but can be regarded as a separate head for recovery. Damages for loss of liberty will increase, the longer the plaintiff has been detained in custody.

Where a plaintiff succeeds in an action either for false imprisonment or malicious prosecution, he is also entitled to compensation for damage to his reputation: the more serious the allegation against the plaintiff, the more serious will be the damage to it. Substantial compensation for damage to reputation will be awarded where the plaintiff's imprisonment has come to the notice of numbers of people, for example:

- where he was arrested in a public place;
- where he was arrested in front of people who know him, for example, at work;
- where he is led through the streets in handcuffs;
- if he is tried in open court but ultimately acquitted;
- where his arrest or prosecution receives publicity in the newspapers, radio and television.

Obviously, the plaintiff is unlikely to obtain any damages for loss of reputation where he has numerous previous convictions.

Reduction for misconduct

Compensatory damages cannot be reduced because of a plaintiff's misconduct or bad character.[8] However, the fact that the plaintiff

---

[8]*Fontin* v *Katapodis* [1962] 108 CLR 177; *Lane* v *Holloway* [1968] 1 QB 379, CA.

has previous convictions may mean the plaintiff has no reputation for which he should be compensated, and his previous periods of time in prison will reduce his mental distress from being kept in custody. The plaintiff's misconduct can be taken into account in considering claims to aggravated or exemplary damages and may reduce or eliminate any right to such damages.[9]

3. AGGRAVATED DAMAGES

Aggravated damages are

"compensation for the injured feelings of the plaintiff where his sense of injury resulting from the wrongful physical act is justifiably heightened by the manner in which or motive for which the defendant did it."[10]

They can only be awarded where they are claimed by the plaintiff, and where there are aggravating features about the defendants' conduct which justify such an award. Aggravating features can include humiliating circumstances at the time of the arrest or any conduct of those responsible for the arrest or prosecution which shows that they had behaved in a high-handed, insulting, malicious or oppressive manner either in relation to the arrest or imprisonment or in conducting the prosecution. Aggravating features can also include the way the litigation and trial are conducted. There can be a penal element in the award of aggravated damages. However, they are primarily to be awarded to compensate the plaintiff for injury to his proper pride and dignity and the consequences of being humiliated. This injury is made worse for the plaintiff because it is more difficult to excuse when the motive is malice, spite or arrogance on the part of the police.

In contrast with basic compensatory damages, aggravated damages can be reduced or eliminated altogether by the plaintiff's own conduct by, for example, provoking an assault.[11]

---

[9]See *O'Connor* v *Hewitson* (1979) Crim LR 46 and *Bishop* v *Commissioner of Police of the Metropolis* (1989) 133 SJ 1626, CA.
[10]See *Cassell & Co* v *Broome* [1972] AC 1027,1124, HL.
[11]*O'Connor* v *Hewitson* [1979] Crim LR 46, CA.

Any evidence which tends to aggravate or mitigate the damage up to the moment when damages is assessed is admissible.[12] This will include attempts by the police to justify their conduct in their pleadings[13] or at trial. Similarly, in *Marks* v *Chief Constable of Greater Manchester Police*,[14] the Court of Appeal held that a chief constable's conduct in continuing to maintain a denial of liability in defence of a civil action, notwithstanding the comments which had been made by a Recorder in criminal proceedings against the plaintiff that police witness evidence was contradictory and could not be relied upon, was arguably capable of aggravating the plaintiff's damages should she succeed in establishing liability in the civil action and could even be relevant to her claim for exemplary damages.

4. **EXEMPLARY DAMAGES**

Claims brought against the police are unusual because the plaintiff will often receive an award for exemplary or punitive damages. This type of damages is contrary to general principle since it is awarded to punish a defendant as opposed to compensating the plaintiff. Such damages will not be awarded for claims arising out of any tort for which damages were not available prior to 1964 including public nuisance.[15]

Exemplary damages can only be given if the sum which is awarded to the plaintiff for compensatory and aggravated damages is insufficient for the purposes of punishing the defendant, showing that tort does not pay and deterring others from acting similarly. It will therefore be regarded as perverse to award exemplary damages but no compensatory damages.[16] The plaintiff must be the victim of punishable behaviour. Awards for exemplary damages must be kept at moderate levels and should not exceed

---

[12]See *Walters* v *Alltools* (1944) 61 TLR 39, 40.
[13]See *Warwick* v *Foulkes* (1844) 12 M&W 506.
[14]*The Times*, 28 January 1992.
[15]See *AB* v *South West Water Services* [1993] QB 507, CA.
[16]See *Cumber* v *Chief Constable of Hampshire Constabulary* [1995] 2 CLY 159, CA.

the minimum sum necessary to meet the public purpose underlying such damages, namely punishment and deterrence.[17]

Exemplary damages will be appropriate if the police are guilty of unconstitutional, arbitrary or oppressive behaviour.[18] They can be awarded against the police as "servants of the government".[19] They may be available if the police simply act unconstitutionally by making a wrongful arrest although it is proper for a judge, when directing a jury that they have the power to give or withhold exemplary damages, to indicate that there are no aggravating or oppressive circumstances.[20] Exemplary damages will not be awarded where the police officers responsible have already been punished by the criminal courts for their misconduct.[21] Where the police assault a suspect in custody, exemplary damages will not be reduced to take into account the plaintiff's criminal record since he is entitled to expect that he will be given the protection of the law in these circumstances.[22]

If the plaintiff has joined individual police officers as defendants in the proceedings, any award of exemplary damages must be awarded by reference to the particular defendant whose conduct is least blameworthy so that the entitlement to exemplary damages may disappear altogether.[23]

The police will be liable for exemplary damages by acting in a arbitrary and oppressive way such as:

- the abuse of their public office by acting unlawfully;
- by assaulting the plaintiff;
- by presenting evidence in court which is held to be false;
- by making a publicly embarrassing wrongful arrest;
- by being guilty of racist or sexist abuse;
- by persistently and aggressively questioning the plaintiff;
- by deliberately subjecting the plaintiff to unpleasant conditions of detention;
- if they are guilty of any deliberate misconduct.

---

[17]See *Cassell & Co* v *Broome* [1972] AC 1027, HL; *Elton John* v *MGN* [1996] 3 WLR 593.
[18]*Rookes* v *Barnard* [1964] AC 1129, HL.
[19]*Holden* v *Chief Constable of Lancashire* [1987] QB 380, CA.
[20]*Ibid* at 389.
[21]See *Archer* v *Brown* [1985] QB 401.
[22]See *Treadaway* v *Chief Constable of West Midlands, The Times,* 25 October 1994.
[23]*Cassell & Co* v *Broome* [1972] AC 1027, HL.

5. ASSESSING DAMAGES: JUDGE AND JURY

The approach to the assessment of damages is fundamentally different depending upon whether the case is being tried before a judge alone or by a judge and jury.

Where a trial is held before a judge alone, it has long been possible to refer him to analogous cases when he is considering the quantum of damages. This has become the universal practice in personal injury actions but has been less common in claims brought against the police. Although the judge is not bound to follow the decided cases, he is likely to find them a helpful starting point in an area of litigation where damages awards are wide-ranging, inconsistent and unpredictable.

In contrast, where the jury assesses damages, there was a long-standing rule of practice that neither the judge nor counsel were able to mention figures of decided cases to them. This has had the unfortunate consequence that jury awards of damages have varied over a very large range.

This problem was dealt with by the Court of Appeal in the case of *Thompson* v *Commissioner of Police*.[24] Detailed guidance was given as to the directions which a judge should include in a summing up to assist the jury on the quantum of damages.

The Court of Appeal said that, although there was no formula which was appropriate for all cases and the precise form of summing up was a matter of discretion, the following guidelines were appropriate:

(1) Juries should be told that, "Save in exceptional circumstances . . . damages are only awarded as compensation . . . They are not intended to punish the defendant".

(2) Compensatory damages are of two types: "ordinary" or "basic" damages and "aggravated" damages. The latter can only be awarded where they are claimed by the plaintiff and where there are aggravating features which justify the award.

(3) Basic damages should depend on the circumstances and the degree of harm suffered but the jury should be given "an appropriate bracket to use as a starting point". The judge

---

[24][1997] 2 All ER 774.

should determine the bracket after having heard submissions from counsel in the absence of the jury.

(4) In a normal case, the jury should be given an approximate figure to be taken "as the correct starting point for basic damages" and should also be given an approximate "ceiling figure".

(5) In false imprisonment cases £500 for the first hour was an appropriate starting point. Damages for longer periods should increase proportionately on a reducing scale with, for example, a plaintiff who had spent 24 hours in custody being entitled to £3,000. For subsequent days the daily rate should be on a progressively reducing scale.

(6) In malicious prosecution cases, the starting point should be £2,000, and in the case of a prosecution lasting up to two years and being taken to the Crown Court an award of £10,000 could be appropriate.

(7) These figures were to assist the judge in determining a bracket within which the jury should be invited to place their award but circumstances can vary dramatically from case to case and the figures "are not intended to be applied in a mechanistic manner".

(8) The nature of aggravated damages should be explained to the jury. Such damages would be appropriate if there were aggravating features about the police conduct.[25]

(9) The jury should be told that if they consider the case is one for an award of damages other than basic damages, they should usually make a separate award for each category.

(10) If aggravated damages were appropriate then the figure was unlikely to be less than £1,000. In the ordinary way the court would not expect the aggravated damages to be as much as twice the basic damages unless the basic damages are modest.

(11) It should be strongly emphasised to the jury that the total of basic and aggravated damages should not exceed what they consider to be fair compensation for the injury which the plaintiff has suffered.

(12) Finally, the jury should be told that if exemplary damages are claimed and the judge considers that there is evidence to

---

[25]See p. 41 above.

support such a claim, damages can be awarded with the object of punishing the defendant "where there has been conduct, including oppressive or arbitrary behaviour by police officers which deserves the exceptional remedy of exemplary damages". It should be explained to the jury that:

(a) if aggravated damages are being awarded these will already have provided some compensation for the injury suffered by the plaintiff as a result of the oppressive and insulting behaviour of the police officer;

(b) exemplary damages should be awarded only if the jury considers that the compensation awarded by way of basic and aggravated damages is in the circumstances inadequate punishment for the defendant;

(c) an award of exemplary damages is a windfall for the plaintiff and, where damages are payable out of police funds, the sum awarded will not be available to be expended by the police to benefit the public (this last direction will be inappropriate if the claim is being met by insurers);

(d) the sum awarded by way of exemplary damages should be sufficient to mark the jury's disapproval of the oppressive and arbitrary behaviour but should be no more than is required for this purpose.

(13) Where exemplary damages were appropriate, they were unlikely to be less than £5,000. The conduct must be particularly deserving of condemnation for an award of as much as £25,000. The figure of £50,000 should be regarded as the absolute maximum, involving directly officers of at least the rank of superintendent. It will be unusual for exemplary damages to produce a total damages award (that is, the total of basic, aggravated and exemplary damages) of more than three times the basic damages being awarded except where the basic damages are low.

(14) In an appropriate case, the jury should be told that even though the plaintiff succeeds on liability, any improper conduct of which they find him guilty could reduce or even eliminate any award of aggravated or exemplary damages.

This made it clear that the figures which had been suggested would, in the future, have to be adjusted for inflation. The Court rejected a submission by the police that the failure of a plaintiff to co-operate in the complaints procedure should reduce damages.

The practical application of these guidelines can be seen in the two cases considered by the Court of Appeal in *Thompson*.

The plaintiff in the first case, Claudette Thompson, had been lawfully arrested but later assaulted by four or five police officers in a cell and maliciously prosecuted for assaulting the police. The prosecution lasted for seven months. The jury had awarded compensatory and aggravated damages of £1,500 and exemplary damages of £50,000. The Court of Appeal held that the compensatory damages award of £1,500 was "totally out of line". They indicated that the appropriate award would have been £10,000 compensatory damages, £10,000 aggravated damages and exemplary damages of £25,000. This would have given a total award of £45,000. As a result, the Court refused to interfere with the jury's award.

The plaintiff in the second case, Kenneth Hsu, was wrongfully arrested, assaulted and racially abused. He was wrongfully held in a cell for one-and-a-quarter hours. He sustained cuts and bruises and a stiff neck. Three years after the incident he was still suffering some symptoms of post-traumatic stress disorder. The jury awarded him £20,000 by way of compensatory, including aggravated damages, and £200,000 exemplary damages. The Court of Appeal said that it would not interfere with the award of £20,000 as compensation. However, the award of exemplary damages could not stand. It was pointed out that "the whole incident was over in a matter of hours and there is already an award of aggravated damages to be taken into account". As a result, the award of exemplary damages was reduced to £15,000.

The awards of damages approved by the court in *Thompson* make it clear that the case is unlikely to depress the level of damages in police cases. The awards to both plaintiffs are still substantial. The "guidelines" are designed to reduce extremely high awards. Such awards are rare, particularly outside London. The guidelines will introduce a greater degree of uniformity and predictability. Their main practical effect is likely to be a "levelling up" of damages to the "standard" level of London awards.

6. ASSESSING DAMAGES FOR ASSAULT

A plaintiff who suffers physical or mental injuries after being assaulted by the police is entitled to recover compensatory damages for his financial losses (such as damaged clothing) as well as general damages for pain and suffering. Damages for assault are probably the most straightforward to assess because it is possible to compare awards in personal injury cases when considering the award for pain and suffering.

The Judicial Studies Board Guidelines lay down guidelines for the assessment of damages in personal injury cases.[26] In *Scotland* v *Metropolitan Police Commissioner*[27] the Court of Appeal stated that it would be proper for the judge, after discussing these guidelines with counsel in the absence of the jury, to indicate figures to the jury. The judge should, at the same time, indicate that everything depended on their assessment of the gravity of the injuries and they were not bound by the bracket which could be a wide one.[28]

7. ASSESSING DAMAGES FOR FALSE IMPRISONMENT

A plaintiff who has been wrongfully arrested or unlawfully detained is entitled to compensation for the suffering he has sustained from being placed in prison, for the loss of his liberty and damage to his reputation as well as compensation for any financial losses such as lost earnings or the cost of obtaining his release. All other things being equal, a plaintiff who has been wrongfully arrested and subsequently detained will recover a higher award of damages than a plaintiff who was initially arrested lawfully but unlawfully detained.

When considering the level of the *"Thompson* bracket" for damages, there are a number of factors to be taken into account including:

- the "quality" of the police misconduct, namely whether it involves a "serious abuse of power" or is only "technical" in

---

[26]See *Guidelines for the Assessment of General Damages in Personal Injury Cases*, 3rd ed, 1996; also in Kemp and Kemp *The Quantum of Damages*, Vols 2 and 3.

[27]19 January 1996, unreported, CA.

[28]See also *Thompson* v *Commissioner of Police of the Metropolis* [1997] 2 All ER 774.

nature. This requires consideration to be made of the circumstances of the arrest, and the length of detention;

- the character of the plaintiff and in particular whether he has previous convictions or has spent periods in prison.

Other factors which will affect the quantum of an award include whether the plaintiff's arrest received publicity in the newspapers or elsewhere, the kind of mental distress suffered by the plaintiff from being falsely imprisoned and any special damages incurred such as loss of earnings as a result of time off work.

Unfortunately, *Thompson* does not give guidance as to the assessment of damages in cases which assess damages where the plaintiff has served a very lengthy prison sentence which was quashed on appeal. This makes assessing quantum in this class of case highly speculative. Some assistance may be given by the amounts awarded by the Home Office as *ex gratia* payments to long-term prisoners released from custody. Application for a payment may be made under section 133 of the Criminal Justice Act 1988 the purpose of which is to provide statutory compensation in cases of miscarriages of justice. Section 133 does not give any guidance as to the principles to be applied by the assessor in assessing the amount of compensation. However, the previous "non-statutory" scheme operated according to "common law principles" and in the "Notes for Successful Applicants" put forward by the Home Office it is stated that the assessor applies "principles analogous to those governing the assessment of damages for civil wrongs". However, the award does not include "any element analogous to exemplary or punitive damages".[29]

In November 1993, a person imprisoned for two years three months as a result of the misdeeds of the West Midlands Serious Crime Squad was awarded £30,000 (or about £13,300 per annum). Another was awarded £55,000 for almost six years (or about £9,200 per annum). A person who was wrongfully convicted of the murder of a police officer and served nearly six years in prison was awarded £90,000 (or £15,000 per annum) in October 1993. At 1997 figures, these suggest a bracket of £10,000 to £17,000 for "basic" damages for long periods of detention.

---

[29]"Notes for Successful Applicants", para. 6.

8. ASSESSING DAMAGES FOR MALICIOUS PROSECUTION

A plaintiff who succeeds in proving that he was maliciously prosecuted will recover compensatory damages for the distress and anxiety he sustained by facing a false charge, for the deprivation of his liberty and for damage to his reputation. In addition, he is entitled to the reimbursement of any expenses or financial losses that result from the prosecution.

Very often a plaintiff will succeed both in false imprisonment and malicious prosecution and the court will be careful to ensure he does not receive a double recovery of damages by awarding overlapping damages. Malicious prosecution damages will be strictly limited to damages which begin from the time the plaintiff was charged and relate solely to his continuing prosecution.

When considering the level of the "*Thompson* bracket" for damages, there are a number of factors to be taken into account including:

- the seriousness of the offence for which he was prosecuted;
- the period of time for which the prosecution "hung over" the plaintiff;
- whether the charge put the plaintiff at risk of being imprisoned or losing his livelihood;
- the emotional distress suffered by the plaintiff from being prosecuted;
- any time for which the plaintiff was remanded in custody or served a prison sentence.

If the plaintiff has previous convictions, this will reduce any compensation he will recover for loss to reputation or for the distress he suffers from being prosecuted.

9. ASSESSING DAMAGES FOR OTHER CAUSES OF ACTION

The particular problems of assessing damages in police cases do not arise where the plaintiff successfully sues for more conventional causes of action and reference should be made to *McGregor on Damages*[30] which is relevant for actions in negligence, breach of statutory duty, trespass to land or wrongful interference with goods.

Damages in relation to goods

Where the police are guilty of trespass to goods or conversion, the plaintiff has a wide range of remedies and damages will differ depending on facts of the case. He may seek an order for their re-delivery or may seek financial compensation only. In either event, the plaintiff is entitled to compensation for any consequential loss such as hiring a replacement or recovering damages for loss of use.

If the goods are destroyed by the police, the plaintiff is entitled to their market value as at the date they were converted. If, on the other hand, they are returned in a damaged state, the plaintiff is entitled to the cost of repair and any decrease of value that results from repair. However, if a repair makes the goods more valuable, a defendant is not entitled to make any deduction from the damages which must be paid.

Compensation for trespass to goods was awarded in *White* v *Brown*[31] where a 72-year-old woman was stopped in a store by the defendant's manager and had her handbag snatched for few moments. She was taken back into the shop and kept for 15 minutes and then taken to the police station for a further 90 minutes. The jury awarded damages of £775 for trespass to goods and £520 for false imprisonment (1997 value: £1,450 and £969 respectively).

Damages in relation to land

Where the police enter the plaintiff's home and damage the fittings and fixtures such as the windows or doors, the plaintiff will recover the cost of their repair. Furthermore, trespass will justify an award of nominal damages although aggravated and exemplary damages

---

[30]15th ed, Sweet and Maxwell, 1988.
[31][1983] CLY 972.

may also be available. For example, in *George* v *Metropolitan Police Commissioner*[32] the police forcibly and unlawfully entered the plaintiff's house to search for her son. They hit and kicked her and ransacked the house. She suffered bruising and tenderness over a number of parts of her body and was awarded compensatory damages for trespass and assault of £6,000 and exemplary damages of £2,000 (1997 value: £6,500 and £2,200). In *Harrison and Hope* v *Chief Constable of Greater Manchester*[33] following a lawful entry police officers conducted an unlawful search and were, therefore, trespassers *ab initio*. Each plaintiff was awarded damages of £1,000 (1997 value: £1,060).

10. REMEDIES FOR THE RETURN OF GOODS

Introduction

There are many instances where the police have taken custody of goods which their owner wishes to recover. During the course of a criminal investigation the police may take goods claiming they may be used as evidence. They may seize goods on the basis that the goods in fact belong to someone else although they are not suggesting that the goods were obtained by criminal means; or they may be reluctant to return the goods because they feel that there are competing claims for ownership.

Where it becomes necessary to seek the return of goods which the police have retained, a potential plaintiff has two standard remedies available to him. He may:

(i) bring a complaint under the Police (Property) Act 1897; or
(ii) seek an order for re-delivery of the goods.

The Police (Property) Act 1897

Section 1(1) of the Police (Property) Act 1897 provides a summary remedy for the return of goods where property comes into the

---

[32] *The Times*, 31 March 1994.
[33] [1995] 3 CLY 178.

hands of the police during their investigation of a suspected offence. The goods will be delivered only to their owner and it is therefore necessary for the applicant to show legal title to them. Consequently, the procedure is of limited usefulness and the Divisional Court emphasised in *Lyons (Raymond) & Co v Metropolitan Police Commissioner*[34] ([1975] QB 321) that applications should not be made in cases where there was a real issue of law or any real difficulty in determining whether a particular person is or is not the owner.

Even if an order is made by the court, legal proceedings in relation to the property may be brought against the successful applicant, provided they are brought within six months of the order (section 1(2)).

An application should be made by taking out a complaint since the applicant is then entitled to his costs[35] unless the police do not object to the order.[36]

Orders for the re-delivery of goods

It is also possible to take High Court or County Court proceedings to ensure the return of property. Under the Tort (Interference with Goods) Act 1977, the court has power to order the delivery up of goods which the police have refused to return. The plaintiff need only show he was in possession of the goods before they were taken and does not have to prove his title as owner.

However, it may be necessary to proceed swiftly if, for example, the police have indicated that they propose to give the property to someone else. Any person can apply to the court for an order for the "detention, custody or preservation" of any property which may be subject to proceedings.[37] It is sensible to apply at the same time for an interim order for delivery up under section 4 of the 1977 Act. The procedure for delivery up of goods under section 4 of the 1977 Act is set out at RSC Order 29 rule 2A. The provisions of RSC Order 29 rule 2A apply in the County Court by CCR Order 13 rule

---

[34][1975] QB 321.
[35]*R v Uxbridge JJ ex p Commissioner of Police of the Metropolis* [1981] QB 829, CA.
[36]*Mercer v Oldham* [1984] Crim LR 232, DC.
[37]RSC Ord 29 r 2; CCR Ord 13 r 7(1)(b).

7(1)(d). Furthermore, an application for an interlocutory order for the delivery up of goods can be made before the issue of proceedings.[38]

Such an application should be made *inter partes* on notice by summons in the Queen's Bench Division supported by an affidavit or by an application in the County Court. Taking such interlocutory proceedings or even threatening them is likely to result in the police issuing an interpleader summons under RSC Order 17 rule 1 or CCR Order 33 rule 6 in order to allow the competing claims to be determined.

A final order for delivery up of property can also be made under section 3(2) of the 1977 Act. An order requiring delivery up is at the discretion of the court and will not usually be made for an ordinary article of commerce of no special value for which the plaintiff can be compensated.[39] The plaintiff can instead seek an order for delivery up giving the defendant the alternative of paying damages for the goods value or simply seek damages.

An application under Police (Property) Act 1897 is only appropriate in a very straightforward case where the owner seeks a speedy remedy for the return of his property. High Court or County Court proceedings are the most effective means of preventing the police from returning the plaintiff's goods to someone else claiming ownership; such proceedings provide the most satisfactory venue to adjudicate between competing claims. The High Court or County Court is also preferable where a plaintiff seeks the return of property which the police assert they need in a criminal investigation.

Under section 43 of the Powers of Criminal Courts Act 1973, when a person has been convicted of an offence punishable on indictment with imprisonment for a term of two years or more and the court is satisfied that any property which was in his possession or under his control at the time of his apprehension has been used, or was intended for use, for the purpose of committing or facilitating the commission of any offence, the court may make an order under the section. The section operates to deprive the offender of any rights in the property.[40] It does not, however, deprive third

---

[38]See CCR Ord 13, r 7(2) and r 6(3) and (4).

[39]*Perry (Howard E.) & Co v British Railway Board* [1980] 1 WLR 1375.

[40]s 43(3).

parties of rights. When property is in the possession of the police under this section the Police (Property) Act applies. However, the claimant must satisfy the court "either that he had not consented to the offender having possession of the property or that he did not know, and no reason to suspect, that the property was likely to be "used" for the purpose of the offence.[41] This places an extremely heavy burden on the applicant and it has been held that a claimant to goods in police possession under this section is free to pursue a remedy at common law.[42]

---

[41]s 43(4)(b).
[42]*Davis* v *Hampshire Police Authority* [1978] CLY 3024.

Contents of Chapter 3

Chapter 3
Initial Steps

1. TAKING INSTRUCTIONS

Introduction

Complaints against police misconduct arise in two quite different situations. Sometimes a solicitor will be consulted where the client objects to police behaviour, although he or she does not face any criminal proceedings. More frequently, the client has been charged with a criminal offence which the solicitor is already handling. In either case the same steps should be taken to pursue the civil claim.

The first difficulty that must be explained by a legal advisor is that, even if the plaintiff is successful, suing the police will only result in an award of damages by way of compensation. Of course, no plaintiff will complain about recovering compensation if the police have acted illegally. But the real objective that most plaintiffs have in mind is that the police should be punished for their wrong-doing. Unfortunately, the only way of achieving this aim would be to make an official complaint or to bring a private prosecution. Either step is fraught with difficulties. Furthermore, even if the plaintiff eventually wins damages, it is extremely unlikely that the police officers involved in the action will be disciplined.

A successful civil action against the police offers the best chance of proving police misconduct. Therefore, if the plaintiff is seeking a public vindication, bringing a damages claim against the police is the most effective way of achieving it. Recognition of this fact probably accounts for the dramatic increase in the number of cases now brought against the police.

Taking a statement

The first step an advisor will take is to interview the client to pre-pare a statement. Even if a statement is prepared for a criminal trial, it will be necessary to prepare a separate one for any potential civil claim. Evidence relevant to a criminal charge very often does not overlap with a civil claim and there are specific areas to investigate which may have no relevance whatsoever to the criminal proceedings.

The statement taken for the civil claim should ordinarily cover:

- how, where and when the plaintiff was arrested, or the incident complained of took place – the full circumstances of this should be covered in detail, including the names and/or descriptions of police officers involved, and their respective roles;
- whether there were witnesses to the arrest and, if so, their names and addresses (if known);
- whether the plaintiff or any companions had taken drink or drugs;
- whether the plaintiff recognised or had previous dealings with any of the officers involved;
- whether the plaintiff was told the reason for the arrest and if so in precisely what terms;
- whether he or she was arrested in a publicly embarrassing manner or was handcuffed and, if so, by whom and for how long;
- if any property was seized, what steps the police took in seizing it;
- whether any property or clothing was damaged and, if so, how;
- the cost of repairing any damage to property and any receipts for their repair or replacement that can be produced;
- if the police entered the plaintiff's home or arrested him at home, whether they had a warrant;
- whether the police acted abusively towards the plaintiff and, if so, who said and did what;
- whether the plaintiff was searched when arrested and, if so, how;
- whether the plaintiff was held in custody at the police station and, if so, for how long;
- whether the plaintiff was told the reason for detention;
- whether the plaintiff was given an opportunity to make representations when detention was being reviewed;
- whether the plaintiff was interviewed and, if so, by whom, in what manner and what was said;
- what the conditions of detention were like. Were blankets and regular meals provided?

- whether the plaintiff was subjected to a strip search or intimate body search or had a body sample taken while in custody;
- whether he complained of an assault while in custody. Did a police surgeon attend?
- the cost of any medical expenses incurred;
- whether he was forced to take time off work and, if so, for how long and what earnings were lost;
- whether the plaintiff has previous criminal convictions and, if so, what these are;
- whether the plaintiff was charged with any offence arising out of the incident;
- whether his prosecution or arrest attracted any publicity and, if so, what publicity;
- whether the prosecution put his livelihood in jeopardy.

It is also helpful to deal with the client's own perception of the reasons for why the police behaved as they did, including any allegations of prejudice or discrimination and any remarks made which would support such allegations.

Photographs and other evidence of injuries

If the plaintiff has any physical signs of injury, it is essential that these be properly photographed immediately, especially if the only complaint is bruising which may disappear quickly.

Some form of medical evidence should be sought at the outset. It is vital that the medical evidence is as specific as possible, since an expert may ultimately be needed to analyse the injuries to say how they were caused.

Unfortunately, if the only evidence of the plaintiff's physical injuries is from a police surgeon's examination in the cells, it is unlikely to be of great assistance for the purposes of a civil action. Of course, the purpose of the police surgeon's examination is not to arm the plaintiff for a prospective damages claim against the police. A report prepared by the police surgeon is unlikely to be penetrating or exhaustive, and even more unlikely to be sympathetic.

The relationship of the civil claim to criminal proceedings

If the plaintiff is facing criminal charges, it will not be prudent to commence any civil claim until the prosecution has taken place. As a matter of practice, he is unlikely to obtain civil legal aid until the prosecution has come to an end. The outcome of the prosecution will be relevant to any potential claim. A conviction in the criminal proceedings will be an absolute bar to suing for malicious prosecution unless the plaintiff was acquitted on part of the indictment or was convicted of a lesser offence.

If the issue raised in civil proceedings is precisely the same as that already decided in criminal proceedings then the civil proceedings are liable to be struck out as a "collateral attack" on the decision of the criminal court and hence an abuse of the process.[1] This doctrine only applies if the issue in question was expressly decided in the criminal case and a challenge to this decision is a necessary part of the proof of the civil case.[2] Where the police have failed to prove in a criminal trial that a police officer made a lawful arrest, this does not prevent them from alleging in civil proceedings that the arrest was lawful.[3]

2. FINANCING THE CASE

Introduction

A solicitor is under a duty to advise the plaintiff about his eligibility for legal aid when pursuing his case. Failure to discuss applying for legal aid whether under the Green Form scheme or under a civil legal aid certificate amounts to professional misconduct and negligence.

Applying for Green Form legal aid

When taking instructions at the first interview, the solicitor will consider whether the plaintiff comes within scope of the Green

---

[1] *Hunter* v *Chief Constable of the West Midlands Police* [1982] AC 529, HL.
[2] *Simpson* v *Chief Constable of South Yorkshire Police, The Times*, 7 March 1991, CA.
[3] *Nawrot* v *Chief Constable of Hampshire, The Independent*, 7 January 1992.

Form scheme and should sign the application form for it. Assuming he comes within the financial limits indicated in the current key card, the plaintiff then becomes eligible for legal aid, advice and assistance up to a limit of two hours' worth of work.

Obtaining an extension in order to provide further assistance or to incur disbursements for reports or counsel's opinion must be done by submitting Form GF3 to the Legal Aid Board Area Office before the limit is reached. The need for the extension and the new limit sought must be justified. An extension will be refused if the plaintiff can already show a prima facie case, in which case he should be applying for a full legal aid certificate.

Civil legal aid

It is advisable to submit the application form as soon as possible. If an offer of legal aid is made, the effect of any limitations or conditions, the need to pay the contributions assessed, and the effect of the statutory charge on any award of damages must all be explained to the client. The impact of the charge is particularly significant in police cases, since High Court juries may assess damages so that only County Court costs are recoverable. The plaintiff may then discover that his damages award is swallowed up by the legal costs of pursuing his action. This can also happen in the County Court if costs are awarded on Scale 1.[4]

Where the plaintiff has been assessed to pay contributions, these may now continue for the duration of the case. Furthermore, the plaintiff is under a duty to advise the Legal Aid Board if there is a change in his means.

Financing the case privately

If the plaintiff does not qualify for legal aid and pays for the case privately, he is obliged to pay costs on a solicitor and own client basis, regardless of the outcome of the case. He is also liable to pay the costs of the police if the case is lost. The plaintiff must be

---

[4]See *Brown* v *Commissioner of Police for the Metropolis*, *The Times*, 24 April 1996, CA.

informed as accurately as possible of the likely cost of starting proceedings,[5] must receive regular reports on costs position, and ought to give specific authorisation for major items of expenditure.

3. PRELIMINARY INVESTIGATIONS

Introduction

Once the solicitor has instructions to proceed with an action against the police and the financing of the case is decided, a number of inquiries will be set in motion. Very often the solicitor will be unaware of crucial information which must be discovered before any realistic assessment can be made about the chances of success and the amount of damages that will be recovered.

Obtaining the custody record and other documents

In order to establish the police's justification for detaining the plaintiff, the custody record must be obtained. The plaintiff and his lawyers are entitled on request to a copy of the custody record. It must be supplied as soon as is practicable although the entitlement only lasts for 12 months after the plaintiff's release from custody.[6]

The custody record will document the grounds for detention. It should be carefully checked to see if the information it contains tallies with the strict statutory requirements for justifying the plaintiff's detention.

The following documents should also be obtained at an early stage:

- the national search record (record of stop and search under PACE, section 1);
- tape recordings of any interviews;
- any prosecution statements served on the client;
- the solicitors' file relating to the defence of any prosecution.

---

[5]See *The Professional Conduct of Solicitors*, (The Law Society) Appendix C7.
[6]Code C para 2.4.

Is the claim time-barred?

In most cases it is unlikely that any limitation problem will arise. The solicitor will have been consulted very shortly after the incident which the plaintiff is complaining about. But sometimes the plaintiff will seek advice a long time after the event, particularly if he wishes to pursue a claim after being convicted or after being released from a prison sentence. There are different time limits for different types of case. An action which consists of, or includes a claim in respect of, personal injuries for negligence, nuisance or any breach of duty (contractual, statutory, or otherwise) must be started within three years from the date of the injury or from the date of the plaintiff's knowledge that the injury was significant and attributable to the defendant's act or omission (Limitation Act 1980, section 11). Even if the three-year period has expired, the court has a discretion to allow a claim out of time in cases involving personal injuries and death.[7]

Claims for injuries arising from deliberate assaults are subject to the ordinary six year limitation period from the end of the act that gave rise to the action.[8]

Claims for malicious prosecution are also subject to a six year limitation period. It appears that time begins to run from the date of the favourable determination (that is, acquittal or successful appeal).

Contacting witnesses

It will be necessary to interview any witnesses whilst their recollection of the incident is still fresh. Any statements they make must be signed and dated so that they may be served under the Civil Evidence Act 1968 if, for example, the witness dies or goes overseas by the time the case goes to trial.

There is no property in a witness and therefore the solicitor is entitled to interview witnesses even though the police have done so. If the police surgeon will be called at trial by the police, it is vital to know what he will say beforehand, particularly since the

---

[7] Limitation Act 1980, s 33.
[8] *Stubbings* v *Webb* [1993] AC 498, HL.

surgeon may give evidence of how the plaintiff was behaving as well as giving evidence about the plaintiff's injuries.

Obtaining expert reports

In most cases the only relevant expert evidence will be from doctors. Even if the only evidence initially obtained is from a GP, a report from a consultant should be considered in order, for example, to deal with how the injuries were caused or whether the plaintiff's time off work was reasonable for the purpose of mitigating damages. A consultant's report will be given more weight as evidence when the case is tried.

The consultant will wish to see a statement from the plaintiff in addition to any GP's or hospital's notes.

Evidence relevant to the claim for damages

Frequently attention will be concentrated on collecting evidence on liability so that the damages claim is sometimes neglected.

It will be necessary to seek evidence of the financial losses the plaintiff seeks compensation for, such as:

- any receipts covering repair or replacement of his property;
- invoices showing any medical expenses incurred;
- if any costs were paid by the plaintiff in defending himself in criminal proceedings, the solicitor's bill he has actually paid;
- evidence of his lost wages such as wage slips and a letter from his employer explaining how the loss has been computed and whether any statutory sick pay has been received;
- if the plaintiff is self-employed, a report from his accountant explaining how his loss of earnings is computed;
- evidence of any state benefits received.

Evidence can also be obtained to support the plaintiff's claim for non-financial losses such as:

- relevant medical evidence;
- evidence of any publicity to his arrest or prosecution such as a local newspaper report;

- any evidence indicating the plaintiff's reaction to his arrest or prosecution such as statements from members of his family.

Obtaining transcripts of evidence in other proceedings

In many cases it will be essential to acquire notes of evidence given in criminal proceedings against the plaintiff. These notes may be useful in cross-examination (if, for instance, there are inconsistencies between the police evidence at the civil trial and what they said in earlier criminal proceedings).

If the trial was heard at the magistrates' court, the clerk should be asked for a certified copy of his or her notes of evidence. Where the trial was heard at the Crown Court, transcripts may be obtained. However, these are expensive and prior authority should be obtained from the Legal Aid Board.

The letter before action

The letter before action will give the police an opportunity to settle the claim without the case proceeding further. They will normally treat the letter as making a complaint. The advantages of pursuing a complaint simultaneously with a damages claim are discussed below.

The letter before action should avoid unnecessary detail because the plaintiff will face cross-examination on any discrepancy between what it says and his evidence at trial. At the same time difficulties will arise where the claim is for wrongful arrest and false imprisonment, since the burden lies on the police to prove that the arrest and detention is lawful. If the police fail to provide a detailed response setting out how they will justify the detention, the Legal Aid Board is much more likely to accept that issuing proceedings is justified. A specimen letter before action is contained in Chapter 7.

4. ALTERNATIVES TO SUING FOR DAMAGES

Introduction

Very often the plaintiff's primary motivation in consulting a solicitor is to see if the police wrongdoing can be punished. However, a civil action against the police is designed simply to recover compensation. It is unlikely to result in disciplinary action even if the plaintiff is ultimately successful. On the other hand, bringing a private criminal prosecution or making a complaint can mean that a police officer who misconducts himself is punished.

Bringing a private prosecution

If a private prosecution is successful against a police officer, he will obviously be punished when the court passes sentence. He will be guilty of a disciplinary offence under the police disciplinary code and will face disciplinary sanctions. The plaintiff will be entitled to seek compensation from the criminal injury compensation scheme. The plaintiff can also rely on the effect of the conviction under section 11 of the Civil Evidence Act 1968 in any civil proceedings.

However, the plaintiff will not be entitled to receive legal aid for bringing a private prosecution and must therefore pay for it privately. The costs of doing so will be high, particularly if it is an indictable offence and the officer elects trial by jury. The plaintiff must prove his case to the high criminal standard (beyond reasonable doubt). Pursuing a criminal prosecution will affect any potential damages claim since the plaintiff must disclose his case. The officer's acquittal may influence the civil jury who eventually hear the damages claim.

Experience shows that juries are extremely reluctant to convict police officers of serious criminal offences. It will therefore seldom be prudent to commence a private prosecution.

Making a complaint

Making a complaint will mean that the officers will be investigated to discover if criminal charges or disciplinary proceedings will be taken. However, a complaint is not intended to cover broad policy issues which concern the direction or control of the police by the Chief Constable or Commissioner.

There is no particular form a police complaint should take. In fact, very often a letter before action is taken to be a formal complaint. It should be made to the relevant chief officer. If a solicitor makes a complaint on his plaintiff's behalf, it should be sent with his written consent.[9]

The complaints procedure laid down by PACE is now rather elaborate. The complaint can be dealt with under the informal resolution procedure, if the plaintiff consents and the chief officer is satisfied that the alleged misconduct does not amount to a criminal or disciplinary charge. The officer appointed to resolve the complaint informally cannot resolve the complaint by apologising on behalf of the officer complained against unless he admits his misconduct. No statements made in the course of the informal resolution procedure are admissible in criminal or civil proceedings.[10]

If the complaint is not handled by informal resolution, the chief officer will appoint an officer to make a formal investigation. A report will be prepared which will be sent to the Police Complaints Authority who will assess whether it is satisfactory.

In the light of the report the chief officer must consider whether the officer should be charged with a criminal offence. If he wishes to charge the officer, the report will be sent to the Director of Public Prosecutions to decide on criminal proceedings. Where a police officer is eventually prosecuted and acquitted, the double jeopardy rule may bar any further disciplinary proceedings.[11]

Alternatively, the chief officer must consider laying disciplinary charges after examining the report. Unless the papers have been sent to the DPP, the chief officer is obliged to explain his conclusions to the Police Complaints Authority who will re-consider whether criminal or disciplinary proceedings will be taken. Laying a disciplinary charge will result in a formal hearing. If the plaintiff is called to give evidence, he cannot be accompanied by his solicitor although he may bring a personal friend.

In certain circumstances the chief officer is obliged to refer a complaint to the Police Complaints Authority.[12] The complaint must be referred to the Police Complaints Authority if the alleged misconduct:

---

[9]s 84(4), PACE to be replaced by s 65 of the Police Act 1996, on a date to be fixed.
[10]s 104(3)(4), PACE; s 86, Police Act 1996.
[11]s 104, PACE.
[12]s 87(1), PACE; Police (Complaints) (Mandatory Referrals etc) Regs 1985 (SI 1985/673); s 70, Police Act 1996.

(i)   resulted in death or serious injury
(ii) constitutes an assault occasioning actual bodily harm;
(iii) is an offence under section 1 of the Prevention of Corruption Act 1916;
(iv) constitutes a serious arrestable offence.[13] In addition, the chief officer has a discretion to refer a complaint to the Police Complaints Authority.[14]

The Police Complaints Authority may also supervise the investigation of a complaint. It will do so if the complaint was mandatorily referred to it. The Police Complaints Authority will also supervise a complaint if it is desirable in the public interest to do so.[15]

The advantages and disadvantages of making complaints

A complaint may result in a police officer facing criminal or disciplinary charges. However, in practice very few complaints are actually upheld. In order to prove a disciplinary offence, the allegations of misconduct must be proved on the high criminal standard of proof.

Instituting the complaints procedure does expose the plaintiff to certain hypothetical risks such as:

• the officer may sue the plaintiff for defamation[16] although the plaintiff can claim qualified privilege so that the officer must prove malice to succeed;[17]
• the plaintiff could be prosecuted for wasting police time.

In the past, running a damages claim in parallel with the complaints investigation, gave rise to the significant disadvantage that the evidence provided by the plaintiff and his witnesses in the complaints procedure would find its way into the papers of the advocate for the police in the civil trial, whereas statements provided by police

---

[13]Sched V Pts I and II, PACE.
[14]s 88 PACE; s 71, Police Act 1996.
[15]s 89, PACE; s 72 and s 73, Police Act 1996.
[16]*Conerney* v *Jacklin* [1985] Crim LR 234.
[17]*Cassidy* v *Cunnochie* [1907] 9 F 112.

witnesses would not be disclosed to the plaintiff or his lawyers. This unsatisfactory state of affairs has been changed as a result of *R v Chief Constable of West Midlands Police ex parte Wiley*[18] which held that statements created in the course of a complaints investigation were not protected from disclosure by a "class claim" to public interest immunity.

One possible tactic for potential plaintiffs is to postpone co-operation with the complaints procedure until exchange of witness statements in the civil action. However, the Police Complaints Authority has power to dispense with an investigation if it believes that the complainant is refusing or failing to make a statement.[19]

---

[18][1995] 1 AC 274, HL.
[19]Police (Dispensation from the Requirement to Investigate Complaints) Regulations 1985 (SI 1985 No 672) (as amended), reg 3(3).

Contents of Chapter 4

Chapter 4
Starting Proceedings and Pleadings

1. DEFENDANTS AND COURTS

Choosing the defendant

There are two types of potential defendants in any police case: individual officers and chief officers. When it has been decided to begin proceedings the first tactical decision is which of these potential defendants to sue.

Police misconduct is, of course, the result of the acts or omissions of individual police officers. These officers are personally liable for their torts and can be made defendants in any action.

However, the chief officer of the force to which the police officer belongs – the Chief Constable or the Metropolitan or City of London Police Commissioner – is vicariously liable for the wrongful acts committed by police officers, including special constables, "under his direction and control in the performance or purported performance of their functions".[1]

Although a chief officer could theoretically disclaim responsibility for an officer who has behaved outrageously, in practice this is very rare, and the chief officer will remain liable even if the actions of his officers are a malicious abuse of their office.[2] The only reported case in which a chief officer has successfully escaped liability is *Makanjoula* v *Metropolitan Police Commissioner*[3] in which an off-duty officer committed an indecent assault, having told his victim that if she did not submit to his advances he would report her for immigration "irregularities".

---

[1]Police Act 1964, s 48(1) now s 88(1) of the Police Act 1996.
[2]See *Racz* v *Home Office* [1994] 2 AC 45, HL (Home Office liable for misfeasance by prison officers).
[3](1989) 139 NLJ 468.

If a chief officer is liable for the torts of one of his officers, then damages and costs are payable out of the police fund.[4] Even if an individual officer is sued, there is a discretion to pay the damages out of the police fund.[5] It appears that this is the usual practice.

If the officers responsible were being "lent" by one force to another, then they are deemed to be under the direction and control of the chief officer to whom they are lent, and he is the proper defendant.[6]

Police cadets are treated as being employed by the police authority.[7] Thus, if misconduct is committed by a police cadet, the appropriate defendant is the local government officer representing the police committee.[8] In the case of a Metropolitan Police Cadet, the Metropolitan Police Receiver should be sued.[9]

There are three principal difficulties which arise in connection with suing individual police officers, in addition to the chief officer:

(i)   suing individual officers is likely to make settlement more difficult;

(ii) if the individual officers are defendants, this may be a tactical disadvantage in conducting the case;[10]

(iii) if there is more than one officer involved, it may lead to a reduction in the exemplary damages award to reflect the behaviour of the least blameworthy defendant.[11]

If an individual officer settles a case this may be treated as admission of liability for the purposes of any disciplinary complaint. He will, therefore, be reluctant to settle.

It is, therefore, preferable to sue the chief officer and not to join any individual officers. In practice, it is increasingly rare for individual officers to be sued. If necessary, they can be joined by

---

[4] s 88(2)(a) of the Police Act 1996.
[5] *Ibid*, s 88(4).
[6] *Ibid*, s 24.
[7] *Ibid*, s 28(3).
[8] *Ibid*, s 28(4).
[9] *Ibid*, s 28(4).
[10] As, e.g., they will be entitled to remain in court throughout the trial: *Tomlinson* v *Tomlinson* [1980] 1 WLR 322, DC.
[11] *Cassell & Co* v *Broome* [1972] AC 1027, HL.

amendment if the chief officer seeks to avoid liability for the officer's misconduct.

Choosing the court

Since the financial limits for county court actions were raised from 1 July 1991, the decision whether to sue in the High Court or County Court has become less critical. Any action which includes a claim for "personal injuries" must be commenced in the County Court unless the value of the action is £50,000 or more.[12] However, there is authority for the proposition that civil actions against the police, even if they include a claim for injuries caused, for example, by assault and battery, are not caught by the rules.[13] Such actions can, therefore, be commenced in the High Court without an endorsement on the writ as required by RSC Order 6 rule 291(f). However, there is, in effect, a presumption that cases with a value of less than £25,000 will be heard in the County Court. The rule is not an absolute one, and the court will have regard to other factors, such as whether the action raises questions of general public interest to persons who are not parties, and the complexity of the facts, legal remedies or procedures involved. The 1991 Practice Direction[14] indicates that claims for malicious prosecution and false imprisonment and claims against the police may be regarded as important, and therefore suitable for trial in the High Court.

Under the recent extension of the small claims limit, any proceedings issued in the County Court on or after 8 January 1996, except for those specifically excluded[15] in which the sum claimed or amount involved does not exceed £3,000, will be automatically referred to arbitration upon receipt by the court of a defence to the claim.[16] The specific exclusions are claims for possession of land and "a claim for damages for personal injuries which exceeds

---

[12]High Court and County Courts Jurisdiction Order 1991 (SI 1991 No 724), art 5.
[13]*Elsworth* v *Commissioner of Police* 2 November 1994, unreported, QBD.
[14][1991] 3 All ER 349, QBD.
[15]See below.
[16]CCR Ord 19, r 3(1).

£1,000". The arbitration rules cannot override the right to a jury trial provided by section 69 of the County Courts Act 1984.

2. PRE-COMMENCEMENT ORDERS

If the claim involves personal injury or death, then the plaintiff can apply for pre-action discovery of documents against any person "likely to be a party" to subsequent litigation.[17] All that is necessary is that there is some connection between the plaintiff's claim and personal injuries.[18] Thus, for example, if a person dies in police custody his executors could apply for discovery of the police documents relating to his detention under this provision.

When such an application is made the police will usually be entitled to their costs. But if the police are at fault, for example, by being slow in replying to a proper request for documents then, in exceptional cases, they may be ordered to pay the costs.[19]

A plaintiff can also apply for pre-action inspection of any property as to which a question may arise in subsequent proceedings.[20] Objects such as police truncheons or police vehicles could be inspected under this provision.

3. PARTICULARS/STATEMENT OF CLAIM

Introduction

The Particulars of Claim (County Court) or Statement of Claim (High Court) must set out all the material facts on which the plaintiff relies. The relevant matter should be stated briefly, succinctly, and in chronological order.[21] Because the burden of proof is often on
the police, this initial pleading may be relatively short. It is important, however, to make sure that the facts pleaded accord with the

---

[17]RSC Ord 27r 7A, CCR Ord 13 r 7(1)(g).
[18]See *Paterson* v *Chadwick* [1974] 1 WLR 890.
[19]*Hall* v *Wandsworth Health Authority* (1985) 129 SJ 188.
[20]RSC Ord 29 r 7A.
[21]RSC Ord 18/7/6.

evidence that the plaintiff will advance at trial. The pleader should avoid emotive language as to the nature of the police acts. Any discrepancy between pleading and evidence is bound adversely to affect the plaintiff's case.

Vicarious liability

Whenever a claim is made against a chief officer of police, the facts which establish his vicarious liability must be specifically pleaded. The following formula is commonly adopted:

> "The Defendant was at all material times the Chief Officer of Police for the [   ] Police Area. The police officers hereinafter referred to were, at all material times, acting under the direction and control of the Defendant in the performance or purported performance of their functions."

Assault and battery

Physical interference with the person is only actionable when it is intentional.[22] Unless the acts relied on are obviously intentional, the particulars/statement of claim should expressly say that the batteries in question were intentional.

False imprisonment

The burden of justifying any arrest or detention is on the police. As a matter of strict theory, the plaintiff can simply plead the fact of arrest and detention and put the defendant to proof, leaving it to the defendant to justify the arrest and detention. However, if the plaintiff intends to advance a positive case he can be required to plead it, or be debarred from advancing it[22a].

Any specific failures to comply with Part IV of PACE should be pleaded in the particulars of claim.

---

[22] *Fowler* v *Lanning* [1959] 1 QB 426.
[22a] *Mercer* v *Chief Constable of the Lancashire Constabulary* [1991] 1 WLR 367.

Malicious prosecution

The burden of proving each of the elements of this cause of action is on the plaintiff. The Particulars/Statement of Claim should, therefore, state that:

(i)   there was a prosecution commenced by police officers;
(ii) that this prosecution terminated in the plaintiff's favour;
(iii) that the police officers acted maliciously;
(iv) that the police officers acted without reasonable or probable cause;
(v)   that the prosecution caused the plaintiff loss and damage.

The plaintiff should give particulars of malice.[23] In most cases this will be a matter of inference from the lack of reasonable and probable cause. It can then be pleaded by stating, after the particulars of lack of reasonable and probable cause, "The Plaintiff will rely on the matters aforesaid as evidence of malice".

Other causes of action

Trespass to land

There are two essential matters to be pleaded. First, that the plaintiff, at the material time, was entitled to possession of the land or premises. Second, that the police officers entered the land or remained there after they had been required to leave.

Interference with goods

The plaintiff must state the value of the goods in question, he must identify the goods, state that they were owned by him or in his possession, and specify the acts which are said to constitute the wrongful interference.

---

[23]RSC Ord 18 r 12(1)(b).

Misfeasance in a public office

The burden of proving all elements is on the plaintiff. The particulars/statement of claim must, therefore, state:

(i)   that the police officers were "public officers";

(ii) that they "misconducted themselves in their office" – either by doing something knowing they had no power to do it or by acting maliciously;

(iii) that it was foreseeable that the plaintiff would suffer loss and damage as a result of this misconduct and that he did suffer loss and damage.

The plaintiff must give particulars of malice[24] and may be ordered to give particulars of knowledge of lack of power.[25] Once again, these can be pleaded as inferences from the circumstances.

Pleading damages

Although assault, battery and false imprisonment are *actionable per se* (that is, without proof of damage), it is usual to include in the particulars/statement of claim, for example for false imprisonment, a paragraph stating:

> "By reason of the matters aforesaid, the Plaintiff has suffered loss, damage, distress, inconvenience, damage to his reputation and loss of liberty."

Such a paragraph is obligatory in cases of malicious prosecution, misfeasance in a public office, negligence or breach of statutory duty.

Special damages

Any quantifiable pre-trial pecuniary loss must be specifically pleaded.[26] This would include matters such as:

---

[24]RSC Ord 18 r 12(1)(b).

[25]RSC Ord 18 r 12(4).

[26]*Ilkiw* v *Samuels* [1963] 1 WLR 991, 1006, CA.

- damage to clothing or other property in the course of an arrest or assault;
- loss of earnings resulting from an arrest or prosecution;
- costs incurred in defending a prosecution.

If possible, detailed particulars of the loss, damage, inconvenience etc suffered by the plaintiff should be given at an early stage. This may be useful to show the extent of the plaintiff's claim for the purposes of settlement negotiations.

Aggravated and exemplary damages

Claims for aggravated and/or exemplary damages must be specifically pleaded in the High Court or County Court.[27] The Statement/Particulars of Claim should, therefore, contain a paragraph, for example, stating that:

> "Further, by reason of the matters aforesaid, the Plaintiff will contend that the actions of the said police officers were oppressive, arbitrary and unconstitutional."

The prayer should also contain a claim for exemplary damages.

Other points

The plaintiff's case is, of course, greatly strengthened if police officers have been convicted of criminal offences in relation to the misconduct alleged. In the High Court such convictions must be specifically pleaded. The Statement of Claim should state that the plaintiff intends to rely on the convictions[28] giving the following particulars:

(i)   the convictions and their dates;
(ii) the court in which the police officers were convicted;

---

[27]RSC Ord 18, r 8(3); CCR Ord 6 r 1(b).
[28]RSC Ord 18 r 7A.

(iii) the issue in the case to which the convictions are relevant.

Although there is no specific requirement that such matters be specifically pleaded in the County Court, it is considered good practice to do so.[29]

Interest must be specifically pleaded in the body of the particulars/statement of claim and the prayer.[30] In cases involving personal injury interest is awarded on damages for pain, suffering and loss of amenity at the rate of 2% from the service of proceedings. In all other cases, including false imprisonment, interest is not awarded on general damages for non-economic loss.[31]

4. THE DEFENCE AND REPLY

Defence

The defence should set out the police case in proper detail. In particular, the defence of lawful justification must be specifically pleaded, the "authority or excuse" being set out with precision.[32] The defence should, therefore, set out the grounds which are alleged to give rise to "reasonable cause to suspect" and all the facts relied on to justify an arrest or detention.

If the defendant wishes to raise any issue of fact this must be pleaded in the defence. If this consists only of simple denials then the police will not be allowed to put forward a positive case at trial by leading evidence, or even through cross-examination.[33] However, in *Hockaday* v *South West Durham Health Authority*,[34] the court accepted the argument that a defendant who has pleaded a general denial of a negative averment, and nothing more, is not in fact precluded from adducing a positive case by way of defence, and may cross-examine the plaintiff with that defence in view.

---

[29]See the *County Court Practice 1996* (Butterworths) Note to CCR Ord 20 r 11.
[30](RSC Ord 18 r 8(4); CCR Ord 6 r 1A): *Ward* v *Chief Constable for Avon & Somerset* (1985) 129 SJ 606, CA.
[31]*Holtham* v *Metropolitan Police Commissioner* (1987) Times, November 28.
[32]*Supreme Court Practice* (Sweet and Maxwell, 1997) para 18/12/17.
[33]*Regina Fur Co Ltd* v *Bossom* [1958] 2 Lloyd's Rep 425, 428, CA.
[34]PMILL July 1994.

Reply

A Reply is not compulsory. If no Reply is served, it is assumed that any Defence raised is traversed.[35] Indeed, there is no provision in the County Court Rules for service of a Reply. It is necessary for the plaintiff to serve a Reply if he wants to raise any new issues of fact in rebuttal of the defendant's case or make any admission to narrow the issues.

5. FURTHER AND BETTER PARTICULARS

Generally

An important part of pleading in all police cases is the request for Further and Better Particulars. The plaintiff will almost always require further particulars of the Defence. The police may well ask for particulars of the Statement/Particulars of Claim.

The function of further and better particulars is to enable the other party to know the nature of the case they have to meet. Both parties are entitled to full particulars of the allegations of fact being made, although not of the evidence which will be led to support them. A request for particulars should perform the following functions:

- limiting the issues for trial – for example, asking which limb of an "and/or" allegation is being relied on;
- avoiding surprise at trial – for example, by asking for all facts and matters that will be relied on;
- tying the hands of the other party – by limiting him to those particulars given.

A searching request for particulars can be of very considerable tactical value. Nevertheless, it is a weapon to be used with care. A detailed request, for example, in relation to the matters relied on at every review of detention under PACE will lead the police to consider this point in detail. On the other hand, a request for "all facts and matters relied on as justifying the detention" will limit them to the replies given. They should then be prevented from calling any evidence of additional facts and matters at trial.

---

[35]RSC Ord 18 r 14.

Parties almost always ask for particulars to which they are not entitled. The reply is then "The plaintiff is not entitled to these particulars" or "This matter does not arise out of the defendant's pleaded case" or something of that sort. Nevertheless, the court will require the particulars to be supplied if a party has consented to an order.[36] Thus, an order for particulars should never be agreed without a proviso to the effect that only those particulars to which the other side is entitled will be supplied.

Further and better particulars of claim

The police may seek to explore the Statement/Particulars of Claim with a request for Further and Better Particulars. The plaintiff should be careful in giving particulars not to say anything which cannot be supported by the evidence. If something happened on a great many occasions, the reply may be "on occasions too numerous to particularise". If the plaintiff is unable to give precise details, the reply may be "the best particulars that the plaintiff can give prior to discovery and/or interrogatories herein is . . ."

The plaintiff should not give particulars of the following allegations:

(i) of a claim that an arrest or detention was "unlawful" – because the burden of justification is on the defendant;
(ii) of an allegation that the reason for arrest was not given.

In general, a plaintiff should exercise extreme caution in the giving of particulars as they may provide hostages to fortune when the case is tried.

Further and better particulars of the defence

In most cases the defence put forward by police officers can usefully be explored by a formal request for further and better particulars. The following particulars should be provided:

---

[36] *Fearis* v *Davies* [1989] 1 FLR 555.

(i)   if the plaintiff was arrested for an arrestable offence, the offence alleged;

(ii)   particulars of all facts and matters relied on as giving "reasonable cause to suspect";[37]

(iii) facts relied on in support of an allegation of knowledge or intention;

(iv) all facts and matters relied on as justifying an arrest or detention.

If a defence involves complex allegations about the relative position of police officers and the plaintiff then a plan should be requested. It is submitted that police should give full particulars of all facts relied on when detention without charge was authorised or continued. These are rarely given. It may be tactically advantageous not to follow up an inadequately answered general request for facts and matters justifying the detention – as the police should be prevented from giving evidence in relation to any matters not pleaded.

A Court will not order the following particulars to be supplied

(i)   of a denial – unless it is "pregnant with an affirmative";[38]

(ii) of a denial of lack of reasonable and probable cause.[39]

Thus, the plaintiff will not obtain particulars of a defence to a malicious prosecution case – unless, as is not uncommon, the defendant avers that there was reasonable and probable cause for the prosecution.

---

[37] *Green* v *Garbutt* (1912) 28 TLR 575.

[38] *Pinson* v *Lloyd's & National Provincial Bank* [1941] 2 KB 72, 85.

[39] *Stapley* v *Annetts* [1970] 1 WLR 20, CA.

Contents of Chapter 5

Chapter 5
From Commencement to Trial

1. **GENERAL POINTS**

The most important stage in the large majority of cases is that between commencement and trial. It is at this stage that the case takes proper shape. Documents are produced, details of the pleadings are obtained and a whole range of skirmishes are fought.

If the plaintiff wins a number of these interlocutory skirmishes the defendant is on the defensive and will often be much more inclined to discuss settlement. On the other hand, defeat in interlocutory battles may demoralise the plaintiff and lead him to consider surrender.

The most important areas are:

(i) discovery and documents generally;
(ii) the summons for directions/pre-trial review;
(iii) payment-in and settlement;
(iv) consideration of evidence and final preparations for trial.

Due to the fact that the burden of proof is on the police in most instances the full nature of their case will often not be clear until the pleadings are closed, further and better particulars have been supplied and discovery has been given. A case should be fully reviewed at the summons for directions/pre-trial review stage in order to determine the strength of the plaintiff's case and the advisability of continuing to trial.

2. **DISCOVERY**

Introduction

In a High Court action, once the pleadings are closed the parties must give discovery by list within 14 days. The list of documents must contain all documents which are, or have been in a party's possession, custody or control "relating to any matter in question" in the action.[1] In the County Court the rules are almost identical except that there is no automatic discovery: actions against the police which will be heard by a jury are not subject to "automatic directions" pursuant to CCR Order 17 rule 11.[2] If necessary, an order for discovery must be made on the pre-trial review pursuant to CCR Order 14 rule 1. The plaintiff can also serve on the defendant a notice to produce any document referred to in the defence or in any affidavit.[3]

Two fundamental questions arise in relation to discovery:

(i)   what is a document?
(ii) how relevant does it have to be to be discoverable?

Documents

Discovery covers the whole range of internal police memoranda, notebooks, files and other written records including information contained on a computer which is capable of being retrieved and converted into readable form.[4] It also covers tape recordings, for example of police radio traffic[5] and video films.[6]

Relevance

A document which "relates to any matter in issue" is any document which it is reasonable to suppose contains information which may enable the party to advance his own case or damage that of his opponent or may fairly lead to a train of enquiry which may have

---

[1] RSC Ord 24 r 2(1); CCR Ord 17 r 11(5).
[2] See r 11(1)(h).
[3] RSC Ord 24 r 10; CCR Ord 14 r 4.
[4] *Derby & Co* v *Weldon (No 9)* [1991] 1 WLR 652.
[5] *Grant* v *Southwestern and County Properties* [1975] Ch 185.
[6] See *Khan* v *Armaguard Ltd* [1994] 3 All ER 545 in which it was held that such a film should be disclosed and made available for inspection notwithstanding that it is relevant to the bona fides of the plaintiff's claim.

one of these consequences.[7] Discovery will not be ordered of documents which are required only for the purpose of cross-examination as to credit.[8] Thus, documents relating to previous misconduct by a police officer can only be obtained on discovery if it can be shown that evidence of the previous misconduct may be admissible as "similar fact evidence".[9]

When a party obtains discovery he gives an implied undertaking that the documents disclosed will only be used for the purpose of the action.[10] This rule may be relaxed or modified by the court in exceptional circumstances.[11] This undertaking ceases to apply after a document has been read or referred to in open court unless the court has ordered otherwise.[12]

Privilege in police cases

A party giving discovery may object to the production for inspection of all documents covered by privilege. Three categories of privilege are likely to be relevant in police cases:

(i)   legal professional privilege;
(ii) public interest immunity;
(iii) informer immunity.

Legal professional privilege

A communication between the defendant and his lawyers is privileged if it was made confidentially for the purpose of the giving of legal advice.[13] Communications between the lawyers and third parties will only be covered by legal professional privilege if the "dominant purpose" for its being brought into existence related to

---

[7] *Compagnie Financiere* v *Peruvian Guano* (1882) 11 QBD 55, 63; *The Captain Gregos, The Times*, 21 December 1990.
[8] *Thorpe* v *Chief Constable of Greater Manchester* [1989] 1 WLR 665.
[9] *Steele* v *Commissioner of Police*, (18 February 1993, unreported) CA.
[10] *Harman* v *Secretary of State for the Home Department* [1983] 1 AC 280, HL.
[11] *Crest Homes* v *Marks* [1987] AC 829, HL.
[12] RSC Ord 24 r 14A; CCR Ord 14 r 8A.
[13] *Balabel* v *Air India* [1988] 2 WLR 1036, CA.

contemplated litigation.[14] Statements or reports made before litigation was contemplated are not privileged. Where there is a right to legal professional privilege, that right is not to be weighed against any countervailing public interest, since legal professional privilege is a fundamental condition on which the administration of justice as a whole rests.[15]

Legal professional privilege attaches to documents whose purpose was the seeking of legal advice in relation to other proceedings. It does, not however, attach to other documents brought into existence for the purpose of those proceedings. This means that the police cannot claim privilege for documents relating to a prior criminal case involving the plaintiff. However, disclosure of documents ordered by a judge in the course of a criminal trial does not constitute a waiver of legal professional privilege in subsequent civil proceedings and if such documents are disclosed they must be returned to the party entitled to the privilege.[16]

Public interest immunity

The police can object to the production of potentially relevant documents on the grounds that disclosure would be injurious to the public interest.[17] Public interest immunity will only be made out where the public interest in preserving the confidentiality of a document outweighs the public interest in ensuring the due administration of justice: see Lord Woolf in *R v Chief Constable of West Midlands Police, ex parte Wiley*[18] where he said that:

> "I consider that when a document is known to be relevant and material, the holder of the document should voluntarily disclose it unless he is satisfied that disclosure will cause substantial harm. If the holder is in doubt he may refer the matter to the court. If the holder decides that a document should not be disclosed then the decision can be upheld or set aside by the judge. ... If public interest immunity is

---

[14] *Waugh* v *British Railways Board* [1980] AC 521, HL.
[15] *R.* v *Derby Borough Magistrates' Court, ex p B* [1995] 3 WLR 681, HL.
[16] *British Coal Corporation* v *Dennis Rye Ltd (No 2)* [1988] 1 WLR 1113, CA.
[17] See RSC Ord 24 r15; CCR Ord 14 r9.
[18] [1995] 1 AC 274 at 424e–g, HL.

approached by every litigant on the basis that a relevant and material document must be disclosed unless disclosure will cause substantial harm to the public interest, the distinction between a class claim and a contents claim loses much of its significance."

The immunity may apply either to a class of documents ("a class claim") on the basis that immunity attaches to all documents within that class, or to a particular document on the basis of its contents ("a contents claim"). Before *Ex parte Wiley*, in civil actions against the police, defendants resorted most frequently to "class claims". The ambit of "class claims" has been severely restricted by *Wiley* in which such a claim in respect of all documents generated in the course of a Police Complaints Authority investigation was rejected.[19] The House of Lords held that although individual documents or their contents, rather than the use of knowledge obtained from them, may be covered by public interest immunity, there was no justification for imposing a general class of public interest immunity on all documents produced by an investigation under the police complaints procedure. Public interest immunity does not, therefore, apply automatically to statements obtained in a complaint investigation. However, in *Taylor v Anderton*[20] the Court of Appeal held that investigating officers' reports formed a class of documents covered by public interest immunity.[21] This is justified first, on the ground that it is unlikely that such reports will be relevant, and secondly on the basis that there is a need for investigating officers to feel free to report on colleagues or members of the public without fearing that their opinions might become known to the persons concerned, and that the prospect of disclosure in other than unusual circumstances may have an undesirable and inhibiting effect on their reports.

In *Gill & Goodwin v Chief Constable of Greater Manchester*[22] the court upheld a class claim to documents which might reveal police methods (the public order manual of a police force). In *O'Sullivan*

---

[19]Overruling *Neilson v Laugharne* [1992] 3 All ER 617; *Hehir v Metropolitan Commissioner* [1982] 1 WLR 715, CA; *Makanjuola v Metropolitan Commissioner* [1992] 3 All ER 617, CA; and *Halford v Sharples* [1992] 1 WLR 736, CA.

[20][1995] 1 WLR 447, CA. See also "Attorney General's Statement on Public Interest Immunity", December 1996.

[21]A point which had been held open by the House of Lords in *Ex parte Wiley*.

[22]*The Times*, 3 November 1992; [1994] CLY 337.

v *Commissioner of Police of the Metropolis*[23] Butterfield J held that a summary of a case created by the police to be passed to the Crown Prosecution Service (Met. Form 151) attracted a class immunity. Following *Evans* v *Chief Constable of Surrey*[24] the judge distinguished between "primary" documentation generated in the course of an investigation such as witness statements, exhibits, entries in police officers' notebooks and forensic reports, and "secondary" documentation, which merely summarised findings gleaned from the primary sources, and made recommendations.

Public interest immunity has been held not to attach to statements made in the course of a police grievance procedure designed to deal with complaints of discrimination made by police officers[25] or to a letter from the Police Complaints Authority to a complainant setting out the results of the investigation into the complaint which is confidential to the Polic Complaints Authority.[26]

When the existence of a "class immunity" is not established by authority, the court must balance the public interest in the administration of justice with the public interest in the proper functioning of the police. The court must:

(i)   determine whether the claim for immunity is prima facie valid; if so
(ii)   determine whether the document is discoverable and would assist the plaintiff's case; if so
(iii) compare the two public interests;
(iv)   if he is in favour of disclosure or in doubt about the public interest immunity, the judge should look at the documents.[27]

Where a valid claim to public interest immunity is established, it is still open to a party to contend that without disclosure he cannot properly present his case.[28] In *Ex parte Coventry Newspapers Ltd*,[28a] the Court of Appeal held that notwithstanding that documents in the possession of the Police Complaints Authority were

---

[23](1995) 139 SJLB 164.
[24][1988] QB 588.
[25]See *Commissioner of Police of the Metropolis* v *Locker* [1993] 3 All ER 584.
[26]*Police Complaints Authority* v *Greater Manchester Police Authority, The Times*, 3 December 1990.
[27]*Air Canada* v *Secretary of State for Trade (No 2)* [1983] 2 AC 394, 398–9, HL; *R* v *K(DT) (Evidence)* (1993), CA.
[28]*Gill & Goodwin* v *Chief Constable of Greater Manchester* (above n. 22).
[28a][1993] 1 All ER 86.

prima facie subject to public interest immunity, that had to be balanced against the public interest in preventing allegedly corrupt police officers from successfully suing the press for damages while the courts disabled the defendants from defending themselves and disclosing police corruption. An order was made that the documents be produced on the basis that it would be repugnant to justice and to the public for them to be withheld.

Where the police seize documents under their powers contained in PACE 1984 the duty of confidence owed by the police to the owner of the documents does not absolve the police from complying with a court order to produce the documents in court.[29]

A claim for public interest immunity in a police case does not have to be made in any particular form but, in general the claim should be made in an affidavit sworn by a senior officer although where there is clear authority to support the assertion that class immunity applies, it is sufficient for the claim to be raised by a responsible official within the defendant's organisation: see *O'Sullivan* v *Commissioner of Police of the Metropolis*[30] where the objection on the ground of public interest immunity was properly raised in an affidavit by a barrister employed by the solicitors' department of the defendants.

Informer immunity

This is a form of public interest immunity. There is a public interest in not disclosing the identity of police informers[31] and the premises used for surveillance.[32] It seems that this immunity only covers "professional informers" and not the identity of ordinary witnesses who make statements to the police in the course of investigations.[33]

Waiver of privilege

Legal professional privilege can be waived expressly. Waiver can also be implied in a number of situations, for example:

---

[29] *Marcel* v *Metropolitan Police Commissioner* [1992] Ch 225, CA.
[30] (1995) 139 SJLB 164.
[31] *Marks* v *Beyfus* (1890) 25 QBD 494.
[32] *R* v *Rankine* [1986] QB 861, CA.
[33] *Tipene* v *Apperley* [1978] 1 NZLR 761, 767.

- when a document is used in cross-examination;[34]
- when part of the document is disclosed on discovery this will constitute waiver of privilege in respect of the whole document;[35]
- when part of a document is read by counsel in open court;[36]

Simply referring to a document does not amount to waiver of privilege.[37] If a privileged document is included on the wrong part of the list of documents, this error can be corrected at any time up to inspection.[38] If privileged documents accidentally fall into the hands of the other party, an injunction can be obtained to stop that party using information from the documents.[39]

The question as to whether public interest immunity, once established, can be waived was considered by the House of Lords in *R* v *Chief Constable of the West Midlands Police, ex p Wiley*.[40] Having cited the judgment of Bingham LJ in *Neilson* v *Laugharne*[41] where he stated, "that public interest immunity cannot in any ordinary sense be waived, since, although one can waive rights, one cannot waive duties", Lord Woolf drew a distinction between the situation where government departments concluded that any public interest in documents being withheld from production was outweighed by the public interest in the documents being disclosed in the litigation, and where an individual litigant was performing the same exercise. With regard to the former he observed that the principle that the courts should have the final responsiblity for deciding when both a contents and a class claim to immunity should be upheld, did not mean that it was for the courts to impose immunity where, after due consideration, no immunity was claimed by the appropriate authority. Acknowledging that practical difficulties did arise in allowing individuals to decide that documents should be disclosed Lord Woolf stated[42] as follows:

---

[34]*Nea Karteria Maritime Co* v *Atlantic and Great Lakes Steamship Corp (No 2)* [1981] Com LR 138.
[35]*Pozzi* v *Eli Lilly & Co, The Times,* 3 December 1986.
[36]*Great Atlantic Insurance Co* v *Home Insurance Co* [1981] 1 WLR 529, CA.
[37]*Tate & Lyle International Ltd* v *Government Trading Corpn* (1984) The Times, October 24.
[38]*Briamore Manufacturing Ltd (in liquidation), Re* [1986] 1 WLR 1429.
[39]*English and American Insurance Co* v *Smith (Herbert) & Co (a firm)* [1988] FSR 232.
[40][1995] 1 AC 274 at 424 e–g, HL.
[41][1992] 3 All ER 617, at 623.
[42][1995] 1 AC 274 at 439b–d.

"In a situation where the courts have already established that a class immunity applies to the documents, it may be appropriate for a chief constable, who appreciates that the documents fall within that class, not to make a decision that the documents should be disclosed without consulting other chief constables and in a case of this nature, the authority and the Attorney General and possibly the Home Secretary as well. However, if having conducted the necessary consultation his decision is endorsed, then it is unobjectionable for the chief constable to make disclosure. The court, if the matter came before it, would act on their views, this being the evidence of those best able to assess the importance of the public interest involved in making disclosure. If their views were that the documents should be disclosed the result of seeking the court's assistance would be a foregone conclusion."

He went on to observe that it was unhelpful to talk of "waiver" in the situation where the balancing of the conflicting aspects of the public interest had not yet been carried out, but that where it had already been determined that the public interest against disclosure outweighed that of disclosure in the interest of the administration of justice it was "inevitable that the preservation of the document should follow so as to protect what has been held to be the dominant public interest".

It is clear that the court should prevent information disclosing the identity of informers from being disclosed – even if the police do not claim the immunity. There is no discretion to waive this immunity.[43]

Police documents

Any documents kept by police officers on duty which relate to the incident in issue are discoverable, These include:

- the police officers' notebooks;
- the "incident report book" kept by uniformed officers;
- the "accident report book".

In relation to each individual case there should be documents such as a charge sheet, notes of interview, statements and so on. If a

---

[43]*Marks* v *Beyfus* (1890) 25 QBD 494.

crime has been reported there will be a crime report – included in a "crime book". The police now have a duty under the PACE 1984 Codes of Practice to compile various records, including:

- records relating to stop and search[44] and the *person stopped* book;
- the record of a search of premises[45] and the *search register*;
- an individual's custody record[46] and the *charge book*;
- records relating to identity parades[47]

In addition, there are large numbers of documents kept at police stations recording day to day activities. These include:

- the *occurrence book* – which provides an overall record of the station's activities;
- the *message pad* – recording telephone messages received;
- the *log of radio messages* – recording messages from officers on duty.

The police also keep a number of records relating to complaints and discipline which may be relevant if issues as to "similar fact evidence" concerning previous misdemeanours of officers are involved in the plaintiff's case. These include, for example:

- a *complaints register* – this is kept by each police force;
- a *discipline book* – showing formal disciplinary action against officers;
- documents relating to previous civil actions – pleadings, judgments, statements and so on.

Specific discovery

The discovery which is given by a party is normally conclusive. The solicitors acting for the police have a duty to examine the police documents for themselves to ensure that full discovery has been given.[48] Nevertheless, a plaintiff who is not satisfied with the

---

44Code of Practice A, para 4.
45Code of Practice B, para 7.1.
46Code of Practice C, para 2.1.
47Code of Practice D, paras 2.16, 2.19–21.
48 *Woods* v *Martins Bank* [1959] 1 QB 55.

discovery given by the police, can make an application for a further and better list of documents or for further discovery of specific documents. An application for specific discovery is made on summons, supported by an affidavit describing the documents sought and stating the grounds for believing the defendant has them and that they are relevant.[49] The defendant may be ordered to swear an affidavit stating whether or not he has the document in question and if not when he parted with it and what has become of it. This should be done by the defendant personally, not by his solicitor.[50]

3. MODE OF TRIAL: JUDGE OR JURY

Right to jury trial

In any case involving an allegation of false imprisonment or malicious prosecution, the plaintiff has a right to trial by jury, provided that the case does not require "any prolonged examination of documents or accounts or any scientific or local investigations which cannot conveniently be made with a jury".[51] If the case does involve the prolonged examination of documents a plaintiff will lose the right to jury trial.[52]

In the High Court an application for trial by jury under this head must be made before the mode of trial is fixed on the summons for directions.[53] Nevertheless, even if the trial has been fixed to be by judge alone, the plaintiff may apply for an order that there be trial by jury and the court has a discretion conferred by section 69(3) to order jury trial in such a case.[54]

In the County Court an application for trial by jury "as of right" may be made at any time.[55] If the application is made less than ten days before the matter is listed for hearing, then the court may postpone the trial on such terms at it thinks fit, to allow time for a jury to be summoned.

---

[49]RSC Ord 24 r 7; CCR Ord 14 r 2.
[50]*Clauss* v *Pir* [1988] Ch 267.
[51]Supreme Court Act 1981 s 69(1)(c): County Courts Act 1984 s 66(3).
[52]*Taylor* v *Anderton* [1995] 1 WLR 447, CA, and see *Aitken* v *Preston, The Times*, 21 May 1997.
[53]RSC Ord 33 r 5.
[54]*Cropper* v *Chief Constable of South Yorkshire Police* [1989] 1 WLR 333, CA.
[55]CCR Ord 13 r 10.

Discretion as to jury trial

In cases which do not involve issues as to false imprisonment or malicious prosecution, the usual mode of trial is by judge alone.[56] Nevertheless there is still a discretion to order trial by jury. This applies to all other causes of action and to malicious prosecution and false imprisonment cases which involve the prolonged examination of documents and so on.[57] Trial by jury will not be ordered in personal injury cases unless the circumstances are wholly exceptional.[58] So where a plaintiff claims damages for personal injuries arising out of an assault by the police, a trial by jury is unlikely to be ordered even where the pleadings give rise to an inference that the plaintiff was also falsely imprisoned; the circumstances must be wholly exceptional to justify the exercise of discretion to grant a jury trial in such circumstances.[59] The similarity between misfeasance in a public office and false imprisonment is not a "determinative factor" in rebutting the statutory presumption against jury trial.[60]

When considering whether or not to exercise its discretion in favour of jury trial, there are a number of factors to be weighed. Factors favouring a jury trial include:

- the public importance of cases involving allegations of police misconduct;[61]
- the fact that the integrity, honour or reputation of the plaintiff is at stake and the charges are grave.[62]

Factors against ordering a jury trial, as a matter of discretion, include the following:

- the fact that the normal mode of trial is trial by judge alone[63] – this factor is usually decisive;

---

[56]Supreme Court Act 1981 s 69(3); County Courts Act 1984 s 66(2)) and see *Williams* v *Beesley* [1973] 3 All ER 144, HL.

[57]*Goldsmith* v *Pressdram* [1988] 1 WLR 64.

[58]*Ward* v *James* [1966] 1 QB 273, CA, and *H* v *Ministry of Defence* [1991] 2 QB 103, CA.

[59]*Hendry* v *Chief Constable of Lancashire* (December 7 1993, unreported) CA, and see *The County Court Practice 1996* (Butterworths) p 59.

[60]*Racz* v *Home Office* [1994] 2 AC 45, HL.

[61]*Cropper* v *Chief Constable of South Yorkshire Police*, above.

[62]*Williams* v *Beesley* [1973] 3 All ER 144, HL, at 147.

[63]*Goldsmith* v *Pressdram* [1988] 1 WLR 64, 68, CA.

- the fact that, when a plaintiff is legally aided, the police are likely to have extra costs due to the fact that jury trials are likely to take longer than trial by judge alone.

An application for a "discretionary" trial by jury can be made at any time in both the High Court and the County Court. Such an application should be made as early as possible otherwise there are likely to be considerable difficulties with listing.

Judge or jury?

The question of whether or not to have a jury trial involves a difficult tactical decision. The role of the civil jury is a limited one.[64] Nevertheless, their presence can make a decisive difference to a case. Their verdicts are notoriously difficult to predict – particularly on the assessment of damages. Nevertheless, overall, juries are likely to be more generous than judges.

In a clear cut case where there are no substantial disputes on the evidence, it may be to the plaintiff's advantage to have the case tried by a judge alone – particularly if he has previous convictions or his case seems to rest on "technicalities". Nevertheless, most cases involve direct disputes of fact between the plaintiff and police officers. In such cases, the usual view among practitioners is that trial by jury is to be preferred.

4. SUMMONS FOR DIRECTIONS/PRE-TRIAL REVIEW

Generally

The general outline of the plaintiff's case and litigation strategy should be clear before the summons for directions or pre-trial review. This is the most important stage for seeking interlocutory orders. It is also the stage when matters such as place and mode of trial are fixed. In the High Court it is the last opportunity to apply for jury trial as of right.[65]

---

[64]See Ch 6 pp 123 *et seq.*
[65]See p 99.

In the County Court the "automatic directions" do not apply to a case to be tried by a jury. However, there are some County Courts which try to apply the automatic directions provisions in any event. If this occurs and until a pre-trial review is applied for, the following directions will take effect when pleadings are deemed to be closed, namely 14 days after service of the defence:

(i)   discovery of documents within 28 days and inspection within seven days thereafter;

(ii)   except with the leave of the court or where all parties agree:

    (a) no expert evidence may be adduced at the trial unless the substance of that evidence has been disclosed to the other parties in the form of a written report within ten weeks;

    (b) any party who intends to place reliance at the trial on any other oral evidence shall, within ten weeks, serve on the other parties written statements of all such oral evidence which he intends to adduce;

(iii) the plaintiff to request a hearing date within six months.

If no request for a hearing date is made within 15 months of the date on which pleadings are deemed to be closed or within nine months after the expiry of any period fixed by the court for making such a request, the action will be automatically struck out.[66] The court has jurisdiction to reinstate an action which has been automatically struck out in this way. However, the court will not exercise its discretion in favour of reinstatement unless the plaintiff can show that he has conducted his case with reasonable diligence.[67] The applicable principles have now been definitively restated by the Court of Appeal in *Bannister* v *SGB plc*.[67]

In most police cases the automatic directions will not, of themselves, be sufficient in any event. In particular, the plaintiff will usually have to apply for a specific direction for trial to be by judge and jury.[68] Where a plaintiff is claiming damages for assault, false imprisonment or malicious prosecution the plaintiff should apply for directions as soon as pleadings are closed seeking the following directions:

---

[66]CCR Ord 17 r 11(9).
[67]*The Times*, 2 May 1997.
[68]CCR Ord 13 r10.

(i)   directions for discovery and inspection;

(ii)   service of witness statement within (say) three months (see page 106);

(iii) service of any expert evidence within (say) three months;

(iv) request for hearing date within (say) four months;

(v)   an order for trial by judge and jury.

In addition, consideration must be given at the summons for directions/pre-trial review as to whether one or more of the following orders is required:

- for interrogatories;[69]
- for specific discovery;[70]
- for the amendment of pleadings or the service of any further pleadings;[71]
- an order that either party supply Further and Better Particulars of the Particulars of Claim or Defence;[72]
- for the preservation or inspection of property;[73]
- for directions in relation to statements made in previous proceedings;[74]
- for directions be given in relation to hearsay evidence;[75]
- that there be a trial of a preliminary issue;[76]
- that there be a split trial on liability and quantum;[78]
- for an interim payment on account of damages.[79]

Split trials

In *Marks* v *Chief Constable of Greater Manchester*[80] the Court of Appeal dismissed the defendant's appeal against the judge's refusal

---

[69]See p 104.

[70]See p 98.

[71]See Ch 4.

[72]*Ibid.*

[73]RSC Ord 29 rr 2–3; incorporated into CCR by Ord 13 r 7.

[74]RSC Ord 38 r 28.

[75]RSC Ord 38 rr 20–34; CCR Ord 20 rr 14–26.

[76–77]RSC Ord 33 r 3.

[78]See below.

[79]RSC Ord 29 r 9; CCR Ord 13 r 12.

[80]*The Times*, 28 January 1992.

to order a split trial on liability and quantum where judicial comments about the unreliability of the prosecution evidence had been made at the criminal trial. The fact of such comments may be pleaded and led in evidence on the issue of damages.

Time estimates

It is important for the plaintiff to be clear as to the time his case is likely to take. As a rule of thumb expect a judge alone to deal with four substantial witnesses a day. Jury trials usually take approximately twice as long as those with a judge alone.

Interrogatories

Interrogatories are questions, answerable on oath, which a party to an action may serve on any other party. Interrogatories may be served in relation to any matter in issue in the action.[81] They must satisfy the test in RSC Order 26 rule 1(1) that they are "necessary either for disposing fairly of the cause or matter or for saving costs". They can now be served without leave.

The onus is on the defendant to apply to vary or withdraw the interrogatories.[82] If the defendant fails to make an application to set aside or vary but does not answer the interrogatories, the plaintiff has to apply for an order that the interrogatories be answered. On the application for such an order, in the absence of an application to set aside or vary, the court need not concern itself with the admissibility of the interrogatories.[83]

In a malicious prosecution case the police could administer interrogatories on the circumstances relating to reasonable and probable cause.[84] On the other hand, the police will not be ordered to answer interrogatories relating to their sources of belief.[85] Nor will

---

[81] RSC Ord 26 r 1; CCR Ord 14 r 11.
[82] RSC Ord 26 r 3(2).
[83] *Tate* v *Durham County Council* [1992] CLY 3523.
[84] *Zychlinski* v *Maltby* (1861) 10 CB (NS) 838.
[85] *Maas* v *Gas Light & Coke Co* [1911] 2 KB 543.

interrogatories be ordered on matters which go solely to cross-examination as to credit.[86]

A considerable amount of debate has taken place over the proper role and timing of interrogatories following the decision of Colman J sitting in the Commercial Court in the case of *Det Danske* v *KDM International plc.*[87] Endorsing the Guide to Commercial Court Practice[88] that "suitable times to interrogate (if at all) will probably be after discovery and after exchange of witness statements" Mr Justice Colman gave the following guidance on the approach to interrogatories:

- they must be essential for the preparation of the case for trial;
- the answers would not appear from further and better particulars;
- discovery or witness statements;
- they must be directly relevant to the issue;
- they must not be oppressive or hypothetical;
- the answers would not appear on cross-examination at trial, unless it is essential to have all the answers in advance of the trial.

In *Hall & Crompton* v *Selvaco Ltd*[89] the Court of Appeal emphasised that the test of necessity laid down by RSC Order 26 rule 1(1) is a stringent one. Sir Thomas Bingham MR stated that interrogatories should not be regarded as a source of ammunition to be routinely discharged as part of an interlocutory bombardment preceding the main battle. The interrogator must be able to show that his interrogatories, if answered when served, would serve a clear litigious purpose by saving costs or promoting the fair and efficient conduct of the action. In that case the plaintiffs' interrogatories which were served before exchange of witness statements or receipt of answer to requests for further and better particulars, were found to be premature and covering ground already or shortly to be available to the defendant. They failed, therefore, to satisfy the test that interrogatories must be necessary.[90]

It is clear that interrogatories will not be allowed in the following situations:

---

[86] *Thorpe* v *Chief Constable of Manchester* [1989] 1 WLR 665, CA.
[87] [1994] 2 Lloyd's Rep 534.
[88] *The Supreme Court Practice 1997* (Sweet and Maxwell) vol 1, para 72/A14.
[89] *The Times*, 27 March 1996.
[90] See also *UCB Bank Plc* v *Halifax (SW) Ltd and Another* (1996) 36 EG 148.

- where the object is to obtain the admission of a fact which can be proved by a witness who will be called at trial in any event;
- when it is clear that no admission can be obtained, for example, where the pleadings show a clear dispute of fact;
- when the fact sought to be admitted is solely within the knowledge of the party applying.

In addition, interrogatories will not be allowed when the questions relate only to evidence and not to the facts that a party intends to prove.

Nevertheless interrogatories remain a valuable tool in the hands of a plaintiff trying to explore fully the nature of the police case against him.

Expert evidence

If the plaintiff intends to call expert evidence he must obtain an appropriate direction.[91] Expert evidence will usually only be required in assault cases – relating to the extent of a plaintiff's injuries, or to the manner in which they are likely to have been caused.

Witness statements

Simultaneous exchange of witness statements will take place in the High Court pursuant to RSC Order 38 rule 2A, for the purposes of disposing fairly and expeditiously of the cause or matter and saving costs. Such a direction may be given even if the parties object. In practice directions for exchange of witness statements are invariably given in the High Court and in the County Court.

The witness statements exchanged may be drafted by counsel. When drafting statements it is important to take the witness through earlier attendance notes, through the letter before action and through all the documents disclosed in the case. Most plaintiffs and other witnesses called on their behalf will not be able to look at their witness statements whilst giving evidence, unlike police

---

[91]RSC Ord 38 r 36; CCR Ord 20 r 27.

officers who can usually refer to their notebooks. It is also important to take each witness through the statements of the other witnesses who may be called on behalf of the plaintiff. This will assist in making the decision as to which witnesses, if any, should be called in addition to the plaintiff. The witness statement should cover all matters relating to quantum, for example, details of pain and suffering and loss of amenity should be given in a case involving an assault resulting in personal injuries.

5. PAYMENTS INTO COURT AND SETTLEMENT

Introduction

The police may pay money into court in an attempt to force settlement.[92] A payment in carries the costs to the date on which it is made, but if the plaintiff fails to "beat" the payment in then he must pay the costs incurred after the period within which the plaintiff may accept the payment in.

In the High Court and the County Court the plaintiff has 21 days after the receipt of the notice of the payment in to accept it.[93]

The payment in is usually one single sum to cover all the plaintiff's causes of action, including interest. A plaintiff may require the notice of payment in to be amended, to apportion the lump sum between the different causes of action.[94]

Statements in open court

Under RSC Order 82 rule 5, a plaintiff in an action for malicious prosecution or false imprisonment who accepts money in court or accepts a payment in settlement can apply to the judge in chambers on summons for leave to make a statement in open court in terms

---

[92]RSC Ord 22; CCR Ord 11.
[93]RSC Ord 22 r 3(1)); CCR Ord 11 r 3.
[94]*Townsend* v *Stone, Toms & Partners* (1984) 128 SJ 659, CA.

approved by the judge. The statement can refer to any other cause of action in the claim, for example, assault.[95]

There is no similar provision in the County Court. However, by section 76 of the County Courts Act 1984, the County Court can adopt the "general principles of practice" in the High Court. In *Honeyford* v *Commission for Racial Equality* [96] Drake J stated that in deciding whether to allow a plaintiff to make a statement in open court, the following principles applied:

- the judge should be slow to refuse leave;
- a factor to be taken into account in refusing leave was the smallness of the sum;
- the judge should not give leave to the plaintiff to make a statement to which the defendant takes a legitimate exception;
- when exercising his discretion the judge can take into account
  (i)   the strength of the plaintiff's case;
  (ii)   the seriousness of the defendant's conduct;
  (iii) the nature of the defence;
  (iv) the amount of the payment; and
  (v)   the fact that payment into court implies no admission.

The defendant is not entitled to insist that the statement should indicate that a payment into court is made without admission.

The police may seek to make it a condition of settlement that there be no publicity for the sum paid. A settlement on these terms does not appear to be contrary to public policy and is, therefore, binding on the plaintiff.

6. **OTHER INTERLOCUTORY MATTERS**

Notices to admit

A party may serve a notice on the other party requiring him to admit for the purposes of the case the facts set out in the notice.[97] If the other party refuses to admit the facts within 14 days in the High

---

[95]RSC Ord 82 r 5(3), reversing the effect of *Smith* v *Commissioner of Police* [1991] 1 All ER 714.
[96]17 April 1991, unreported.
[97]RSC Ord 27 r 2; CCR Ord 20 r 2.

Court and seven days in the County Court after service of the notice on him and they are proved at trial, then he must bear the costs of proving these facts, whatever the outcome of the trial.[98]

The purpose of such a notice is twofold. Firstly, it can save the plaintiff the trouble and expense of calling witnesses to prove facts which are not really in issue. The defendant will be put in the position of either admitting the facts or having to pay the costs of proving them even if he is successful. Secondly, a notice to admit facts may serve to prepare the ground for an application for judgment on admissions.[99]

Judgment before trial

In many police cases, the burden is on the police to justify their actions. In theory, if the defence fails to disclose a proper justification the plaintiff could seek summary judgment. There are, however, two objections to such a course:

- summary judgment is not available in cases of false imprisonment or malicious prosecution;[100]
- if the application fails, the police are put on notice of weaknesses in their case and have time to rectify them.

Summary judgment is, however, available in cases involving trespass to land or wrongful interference with goods.

Where admissions of fact are made by the police either in their pleadings or as the result of a notice to admit in the High Court, the plaintiff can, in theory, apply for judgment on admissions.[101] This procedure applies in cases of malicious prosecution and false imprisonment. Thus, for example, if the defence states that the plaintiff was arrested for assaulting a police officer in the execution of his duty (which is not an arrestable offence)[102] then the plaintiff could apply for judgment on admissions. However, there is no corresponding rule in the County Court save where the defendant

---

[98]RSC Ord 62 r 6(7); CCR Ord 20 r2(2).
[99]See below.
[100]RSC Ord 14 r 1(2); CCR Ord 9 r 4(1)(c).
[101]RSC Ord 27 r 3.
[102]See p 10.

admits liability for part of the claim.[103] In practice, therefore, such applications will be rare.

7. PREPARING FOR TRIAL

Re-assessing the case

After all the interlocutory steps in a case have been completed, the plaintiff's advisors should be in a position to re-assess the strength of his case. In legally aided matters this is usually done by having an advice on "merits, evidence and quantum".

The strength of the police defence should be considered. In some cases it will become clear that the plaintiff's case is not strong enough to take to trial. In other cases, it will be apparent that further evidence or amendment of the pleadings is required. The position should be carefully considered with the plaintiff at this stage.

Advice on evidence

It is of the utmost importance to give full consideration to the evidence that the plaintiff will need, in good time for the trial. If counsel is being instructed he should be asked to advise on evidence. If a solicitor advocate is acting, he should engage in a similar exercise for his own benefit. Such an advice should cover the following points:

- *Pleadings.* Are they complete, are any amendments required?
- *Issues.* What issues do the pleadings disclose, what evidence is required on each issue?
- *Witnesses.* What witnesses are required on behalf of the plaintiff? Have draft witness statements been prepared for each witness? Have all the witness statements been exchanged? Will the service of a subpoena be necessary in relation to any witness?
- *Other Evidence.* Is it advantageous to serve a notice to admit? Are any Civil Evidence Act notices required?

---

[103]See CCR Ord 9.

- *Expert Evidence.* Has the plaintiff obtained suitable medical evidence?
- *Documents.* Have the police given full and proper discovery? Which documents are to be included in the bundle?
- *Directions.* Are any further directions required?
- *Photographs and plans.* Are these required? If the trial is with a jury are sufficient copies available?

Witnesses and bundles

The plaintiff's witnesses will have signed their witness statements. They should retain a copy of their statement and be warned of the trial date well in advance. If a witness will not attend court of his own free will, consideration should given as to whether it is necessary to issue a subpoena[104] or witness summons.[105] If the witness is required to bring documents then a subpoena *ad testificandum* should be served. Subpoenas must be served personally and the witnesses offered "conduct money" to cover their costs in coming to court.

It is for the plaintiff to prepare bundles of documents for trial. Five copies of a chronological (earliest first), paginated (page numbers rather than document numbers) and an indexed trial bundle should be prepared containing the following sections:

(i)   Pleadings and orders;
(ii) Documents: all the disclosed documents in both lists (omitting duplicated documents and the procedural solicitor correspondence);
(iii) Evidence:
    (a)   Witness statements: the plaintiff's first followed by the defendant's;
    (b)   Experts' reports: again the plaintiff's first followed by the defendant's.

These bundles should be agreed with the defendant if possible. Careful consideration should be given to the contents of such

---

[104]RSC Ord 38 r 14.
[105]CCR Ord 20 r 12.

bundles. It is helpful for transcripts of the relevant extracts of the police officer's notebooks and of the custody record to be prepared and included in the bundle. In addition, it will be necessary to prepare a "jury bundle". Twelve copies should be prepared in the High Court and eight in the County Court. The "jury bundle" is normally very small, containing only the essential documents for the case. The bundle should contain documents such as:

- the letter before action and the reply to this;
- the custody record;
- the charge sheet;
- agreed plans or photographs;
- agreed medical reports;
- statements served under the Civil Evidence Act.

The bundle should not contain:
- police notebooks;
- police reports into the incidents in question setting out the police version of events.

These documents are hearsay and are not admissible in evidence unless allegations of recent fabrication are being made. Bundles of such documents should, however, be prepared for the purposes of cross-examination. The jury bundle should also be agreed with the defendant if possible.

Contents of Chapter 6

Police Actions

Chapter 6
The Trial

1. PROCEDURE IN JURY TRIALS

Introduction

Actions brought against the police are one of the few areas of civil litigation which are frequently tried before juries. In cases involving allegations of wrongful arrest, false imprisonment and malicious prosecution, the plaintiff is entitled to a jury trial as of right.[1]

However, civil jury trials are often unfamiliar territory except for those who regularly deal with libel and slander or police actions. This often means that judges as well as advocates are uncertain about procedural questions and that practices will differ from one court to another.

Confusion about how to present a case often arises because of the different roles of the judge and jury. The jury decides disputed issues of fact and assesses damages. The judge rules on issues of law. The distinction is straightforward in principle but often creates difficulties during the course of a trial.

Preliminary applications

Normally the trial judge will ask whether he should hear any applications before the jury is empanelled. For example, if there are disputes about the admissibility of documents that would otherwise be in the bundle or a question arises concerning compliance with a direction to disclose an expert's report, the judge will decide these before the case formally commences.

Frequently, applications will be made to exclude police officers from the courtroom until they give their evidence. The application

---
[1]See p 99.

115

must be made before the jury is empanelled. Unlike criminal trials the usual practice in a civil case is that witnesses will remain in court throughout all the evidence. However, allowing witnesses to hear the evidence will give them the opportunity to provide corroborative evidence on any points that arise out of cross examination.

It is simply a matter of the judge's discretion whether he will order the witnesses to be excluded from the court (or from not leaving the court again after giving evidence so as to communicate to other witnesses). However, the court will not exclude parties to the proceedings or expert witnesses.[2] Of course if the individual police officers have been joined as defendants, no application to exclude them from the hearing can therefore be made.

Empanelling the jury

The first formal step in the trial will be the swearing in of the jury. In the High Court there will be 12 jurors. In the County Court there will be eight jurors.

There is no right of pre-emptory challenge to a juror. However, in principle both parties can challenge for cause by:

- a challenge to the array, that is, to the whole panel of jurors;
- a challenge to the polls, that is to an individual juror.

In practice, challenging the jury will very seldom arise.

A challenge to the array involves a challenge to the whole panel of jurors. Such a challenge can only be made if it can be demonstrated that the officer who summoned was biased or acted improperly.

An individual juror can be challenged by a challenge to the polls. It must be proved that the juror is not qualified or biased or reasonably suspected of bias. If there is some prima facie evidence of bias, the juror can be examined on oath.

The right to begin

The plaintiff's advocate will always have the right to begin in a trial where both liability and damages are contested. Even if the burden

---

[2] *Tomlinson* v *Tomlinson* [1980] 1 WLR 322, DC.

of proof on all issues lies on the defendant (as in, for example, a case where the only issue is the plaintiff's false imprisonment claim), the plaintiff should open because he must still prove damages.[3-4]

Opening the case

Once the jury is sworn in the plaintiff's advocate should give an opening speech and explain:

- the background to the case;
- the nature of the causes of action the plaintiff is bringing, the nature of the damages the plaintiff seeks (including, if relevant, exemplary damages) and the role of the judge and jury in deciding them.
- the disputes of fact that arise on the pleading;
- and the documents that comprise the agreed bundle;
- the issues that have to be decided between the parties.

There are a number of unusual features to police cases which ought to be made clear to the jury.

After discussing the nature of a false imprisonment or malicious prosecution claim, the jury should be told about the limited nature of the role they perform. They will not be required to decide in broad terms whether the police are guilty or not guilty of acting illegally. Instead they will be asked to answer a number of specific yes/no questions if the plaintiff and the police give different versions of the event and the judge decides that it is necessary to determine which version of events is true. They should also be told that they alone will be left to assess damages if the plaintiff is successful and that they may be asked to consider awarding exemplary damages if they think the police have acted unconstitutionally, arbitrarily or oppressively.

Furthermore, it is not customary for the jury to see the pleadings in the case so that their purpose must be explained when taking the judge through the pleadings. In the past, the practice was to show

---

[3-4]*Chapman* v *Rawson* [1846] 8 QB 673 and see *McGregor on Damages* 15th edn, (Sweet and Maxwell, 1988).

pleadings to a civil jury but this is no longer conventional. Nevertheless, the jury should be told of the specific grounds on which the police rely when justifying an arrest or detention or that the plaintiff relies upon in alleging there was a lack of reasonable and probable cause for bringing a prosecution.

Calling evidence on behalf of the plaintiff

There are no special factors in jury cases that affect how the evidence will be presented. The plaintiff and any other witnesses will give evidence in chief, be cross-examined and be re-examined in the usual way.

Submissions of no case to answer

In jury trials the judge has a discretion as to whether to put the defendant to his election.[5] If the defendant elects not to call any evidence and the submission of no case is unsuccessful the defendant will not be permitted to continue to defend the claim. If the defendant wishes to make a submission of no case to answer in a jury trial, he will usually wait until the end of his own evidence to do so.[6] However, a submission of no case will only succeed if it can be shown that no case has been established in law for the defendant to answer or where the evidence is so unsatisfactory or unreliable that the court should rule that the burden of proof on the plaintiff has not been discharged.[7]

Even if the submission succeeds, the Court of Appeal has suggested that the jury's verdict should be taken in case the judge's ruling is reversed on appeal.[8] Notwithstanding this the usual practice is that the jury will be discharged without being asked to give a verdict.[9]

---

[5] *Young* v *Rank* [1950] 2 KB 510, 513.
[6] *Payne* v *Harrison* [1961] 2 QB 403, 413, CA.
[7] *Yuill* v *Yuill* [1945] P 15, CA.
[8] *Halliwell* v *Venables* [1930] LJKB 353.
[9] *Young* v *Rank* [1950] 2 KB 510, 514.

The defendant's opening speech

In the High Court the defendant's advocate has a right to give an opening speech before any evidence is called.[10] Such a right is particularly valuable in a case which is factually complicated and where the evidence will be lengthy.

On the other hand, in the County Court the defendant's advocate is not entitled to give two speeches as of right. It is a matter of discretion for the trial judge whether to allow the advocate to give a speech when both opening and closing his case.[11] In practice the usual procedure will be that the plaintiff will open the case and the defendant will make a closing speech only.

Calling evidence on behalf of the defendant

Evidence will be received in the normal manner so that the defendant's witnesses will give their evidence in chief, be cross examined and be re-examined.

Rulings by the judge

During the course of the proceedings the judge may be required to give rulings on the admissibility of evidence. Civil actions against the police are governed by the same rules of evidence as those applying to any civil trial. For example, applications can be made to admit hearsay evidence under the Civil Evidence Acts 1968 and 1972. However, there are particular disputes concerning the admissibility of evidence that occur regularly in police cases.

Evidence of convictions under the Civil Evidence Act 1968

In contrast to a criminal trial no special rules prevent the disclosure of previous convictions of the plaintiff or any other witness. The

---

[10]RSC Ord 35 r 7(4).
[11]See *The County Court Practice* (Butterworths) CCR Ord 22 r 5A and Notes to Ord 21 r 2, p 321.

judge cannot prevent cross-examination concerning previous convictions if they are relevant to a witness' credit. However, if the convictions are spent under the Rehabilitation of Offenders Act 1974, they can only be raised if an application is made under section 7(3) of that Act and the judge:

> "is satisfied, in the light of any circumstances which appear to . . . [him] to be relevant . . . that justice cannot be done in the case except by admitting [the spent conviction]."

Under this section the judge could admit evidence as to previous spent convictions not only if they were relevant to an issue in the case, but also if they were relevant merely as to credit. However, the judge should weigh the degree of relevance against the amount of prejudice caused by admitting the conviction.[12]

If a conviction is properly admissible but it is denied by the witness, it may then be proved.[13] The police should be asked to have copies of the previous convictions of any witnesses they intend to call at court. If they refuse to do this an appropriate order should be sought. An application to see these convictions should then be made at the conclusion of the witness' evidence in chief.

Occasionally a conviction may be directly relevant to an issue in the case. This would occur if an officer had been convicted of an offence against the plaintiff. It would also arise in a case where the plaintiff's only cause of action is false imprisonment and the police seek to justify a wrongful arrest by relying on grounds which formed the basis for the plaintiff's conviction. It is clear that if the plaintiff brings a civil action which seeks to reopen an issue which has already been decided in a previous criminal trial it is liable to be struck out as an abuse of the process of the court on the grounds that it is a "collateral attack".[14] The decision in *Simpson* v *Chief Constable of South Yorkshire*[15] has helped to define the boundaries of the doctrine. The Court of Appeal held that it did not necessarily follow from the plaintiff's conviction for throwing a rock at two police officers during a miner's strike that he would fail to prove

---

[12]*Thomas* v *Commissioner of Police* [1997] 1 All ER 747.
[13]See s 6, Criminal Procedure Act 1865.
[14]*Hunter* v *Chief Constable of the West Midlands Police* [1982] AC 529, HL.
[15]*The Guardian*, 13 March 1991, CA.

that he had been assaulted by police officers himself. The defendant's argument that the plaintiff should be prevented from relitigating the issues in the criminal trial by pursuing his claim for assault therefore failed. Furthermore, the majority of the Court of Appeal rejected a broad brush approach and expressly disapproved of the view that the principles established by *Hunter* v *Chief Constable of the West Midlands Police* applied to inferential as well as express findings of fact even where that inference was inescapable. It is therefore submitted that an action should only be struck out if it necessarily involves the reopening of an issue which is identical to one expressly decided by a criminal court. If no express ruling on the issue was made in the course of the criminal trial, the civil action should be allowed to proceed. Conversely, if the civil action directly challenges a clear decision made in the criminal case, the action will be struck out unless "fresh evidence" has become available which "entirely changes the aspect of the case".[16]

Evidence in other proceedings

The evidence in previous proceedings is only relevant if it shows that a witness's evidence at the civil trial is different from what was said previously at an earlier criminal trial. Such evidence is obviously not admissible to buttress the witness's case by showing that he has remained consistent in the way he puts forward his version of events. The one crucial instance when a previous consistent statement is admissible is when a witness is cross-examined on the basis that he recently fabricated the evidence he is giving.

Police notebooks, statements made and reports prepared for the purpose of any criminal trial will all contain previous statements covering the very same issues as those which arise in the civil trial. All these documents can be put in cross-examination (and admitted as evidence if necessary) during trial. Although these documents should not be part of the agreed bundle to be put before the jury, sufficient copies should be available to be put in evidence if the witness disputes them. In some cases a transcript of the evidence in

---

[16] *Hunter* v *Chief Constable of the West Midlands Police* [1982] AC 529, at 545c, HL; *Colman-Archer* v *Chief Constable of Norfolk* (9 July 1996, unreported), CA.

the previous proceedings will be available. In the High Court notice of the intention to give evidence about statements made in the criminal trial must be served on the police.[17] This will enable them to apply for the court to directions as to admissibility of the transcript.[18] Unfortunately, experience shows that even when the accuracy of the transcript of the criminal proceedings can be proved, disputes will arise with police witnesses about the accuracy of the note.

Similar fact evidence

In principle, either party in civil proceedings can call similar fact evidence. For example, the plaintiff may wish to show that the particular police officers have been guilty of similar misconduct on an earlier occasion whereas the police might wish to adduce evidence that the plaintiff has made previous unfounded allegations. The judge will admit similar fact evidence if it is relevant provided that it is not oppressive or unfair to the other side and that they are in a position to deal with it.[19] In *Steele v Commissioner of Police*[20] the plaintiffs sought discovery of documents relating to allegations of corruption and fabrication of evidence by a police officer whose evidence had been disbelieved on appeal against their convictions to the Court of Appeal. It was held that the fact that a police officer was prepared to pervert the course of justice on other occasions made it more probable that he did so in that case. Beldam LJ said

> "conduct of this kind is so contrary to the expected standard of behaviour of an investigating police officer that, if proved, it is capable of rendering it more probable that the plaintiff's alleged confessions were not made and proving that [the officer in the case] had no sufficient belief in the grounds of and an improper motive for the prosecution of the plaintiffs".

However, Beldam LJ prefaced the above statement with the observation that the significance of the misconduct alleged went beyond

---

[17]RSC Ord 38 r 21.
[18]RSC Ord 38 r 28.
[19]See *Mood Music Publishing Co v de Wolfe* [1976] Ch 119, 127, CA.
[20]18 February 1993, unreported, CA.

mere propensity. In practice whether or not evidence of previous misconduct will be admitted as "similar fact" evidence will depend upon whether, if accepted, that evidence will show that the police officer concerned has previously behaved in a way which makes it more probable that he did so on the occasion in question.

Excluding evidence in civil trials

The trial judge has a general discretion to exclude evidence in a civil case if it is oppressive or unfair. Therefore, where a plaintiff who alleged that the defendant had forged a document which was the subject of the action and wished to call evidence that he had forged other documents on previous occasions, the judge ruled that he had a discretion to exclude some of that evidence because it was oppressive and unfair to admit it.[21]

In the course of the trial the judge will normally give a ruling, for example, on whether the police had reasonable cause to suspect the plaintiff or whether the plaintiff can prove an absence of reasonable and probable cause in the police bringing the prosecution.

Rulings will not normally be made in the presence of the jurors so that an application should be made for the jury to leave the court when a ruling is sought.

Is there a case to go before the jury?

After all the evidence is heard, it is common to make an application that there is not a case that is fit to go before the jury.

Either advocate can make such an application if the other sides' case, taken at its highest, would not discharge the burden of proof that they must meet. For example, it is possible in wrongful arrest cases to submit that, even if the police are believed on all the disputes of fact, their evidence would still not amount to proof of reasonable cause for suspicion. The defendant's advocate can likewise argue in a malicious prosecution case that the evidence put

---

[21] *Berger* v *Raymond Sun* [1984] 1 WLR 625.

forward is insufficient, even if believed in its totality, of amounting to the absence of reasonable and probable cause or of malice.

The role of the jury is to determine issues of fact which are disputed and which require resolution before the judge can make rulings on the law. The issues of the reasonableness of the suspicions or beliefs of police officers are matters for the judge alone. It follows, that if there are no relevant disputes of fact the judge need not seek the determination of the jury.[22] In that instance the judge may rule that there are no issues to be decided by the jury and he will then proceed to make a ruling on reasonable and probable cause immediately after the conclusion of the evidence.

An application by the plaintiff that the evidence is insufficient to justify false imprisonment will have very few advantages. It deprives the jury of the opportunity of deciding any disputes of fact which could ultimately favour the plaintiff. If the police successfully appeal the judge's ruling, at best the Court of Appeal must be persuaded to order a new trial on liability. Sometimes they will refuse to do so. Even if the case is set down for a new trial, the plaintiff is at risk of being ordered to pay the costs of the first trial and the appeal. The costs would be deducted from any damages he eventually wins, even if he is legally aided.

The more cautious approach is to let the disputes of fact be determined by the jury. Even if the defendant's case is accepted in its entirety, the plaintiff is no worse off. He is in the same position when seeking the judge's ruling as if he had made a submission that there was no case fit to go before the jury but he is not at risk of facing a successful appeal with the problems discussed earlier.

Formulating questions for the jury

At the close of the evidence the judge will seek the assistance of the advocates about the form of the questions to be put to the jury. The judge usually expects the draft questions to be prepared by the advocates. He will prefer the draft questions to be agreed. Nevertheless, the judge himself will decide the form of the wording after hearing argument.

---

[22] *Kelly* v *Chief Constable of Hampshire, The Independent*, 25 March 1993.

The Trial

The form of the jury questions often generates great confusion and what is assumed to be good practice is sometimes legally incorrect. The most authoritative statement of the role of the jury and the nature of the questions they should be asked is contained in *Dallison* v *Caffery*.[23] It is a case which should be brought to the hearing since the nature of the jury questions is so frequently misunderstood. The approach set out by Diplock LJ[24] is as follows:

"It is a well-settled rule of procedure that the question of whether [the police are acting reasonably in arresting, detaining or prosecuting a suspect] is one to be decided by the judge. . . . It is for judge to decide what facts given in evidence are relevant to the question of whether the defendant acted reasonably. It is thus for him to decide, in the event of a conflict of evidence, what finding of fact is relevant and requisite to enable him to decide that question. But a jury is entitled to base findings of fact only on the evidence called before it and, as in any other jury trial, it is for the judge in an action for false imprisonment or malicious prosecution to decide whether the evidence on a relevant matter does raise an issue of fact fit to be left to the jury. If there is no real conflict of evidence, there is no issue of fact calling for a determination by the jury. This applies not only to issues of fact as to what happened, on which the judge has to base his determination whether the defendant acted reasonably, but also to the issue of fact whether the defendant acted honestly, which if there is sufficient evidence to raise this issue, is one for the jury. (See *Herniman* v *Smith* [1938] AC 305.) . . . however, where there is reasonable and probable cause for an arrest or prosecution, the judge should not leave this issue to the jury except in the highly unlikely event that there is cogent positive evidence that, despite the actual existence of reasonable and probable cause, the defendant himself did not believe that it existed: see *Glinski* v *McIver* [1962] AC 726."

Unfortunately, questions which are sometimes used and which are assumed to constitute good practice do not comply with Diplock LJ's remarks. For example, one type of question often put before a jury in a case involving a wrongful arrest and malicious prosecution for theft is:

---

[23][1965] 1 QB 348, CA.
[24]At pp 371, 372.

125

"Did the defendant have reasonable grounds to suspect the plaintiff was guilty of theft?"

Another example is:

"On the issue of malicious prosecution do you find for the plaintiff or the defendant?"

The objection to both these jury questions is that they require the jury to decide that the defendant is guilty of wrongful arrest or malicious prosecution. However, it is plain beyond argument that the judge must decide the question of reasonable and probable cause in both false imprisonment and malicious prosecution cases[25] so that both these questions amount to errors of law.

The correct approach is to formulate a number of specific yes/no questions arising from disputed issues of fact. The judge will then hear argument from the advocates about whether the various jury findings taken together amount to reasonable and probable cause. The normal practice is to draft:

- separate questions for each assault alleged;
- separate questions for each of the grounds which are relied upon for proving reasonable and probable cause which will normally be the individual particulars set out in the pleadings;
- questions dealing with the subjective belief of the police officer, assuming there is evidence that despite the existence of the above grounds, the officer himself did not believe them.

When the burden of proof shifts, the jury questions should fall into two sections, for example:

(i) has the defendant satisfied you of the following facts (which are then enumerated); and

(ii) has the plaintiff satisfied you of the following facts.

This may be appropriate, for example, where the plaintiff has to prove he was assaulted whereas the police must prove they used reasonable force.

---

[25]See *Lister* v *Perryman* [1870] LR 4 HL 521.

The Trial

It is comparatively rare that the jury will be asked questions about the subjective belief of police officers. In most cases the police version of events will be disputed and the jury will simply decide what happened. If the police evidence of the events is disbelieved, it follows that they could not have genuinely believed those events took place.

On the other hand, there will be occasions when the grounds for the police's belief may exist independently of what actually occurred. For example, the plaintiff may claim that even if the police had reasonable grounds to justify their actions, they acted out of an improper motive in order, for example, to harass him. In such a case it will be essential for the jury to decide whether or not the police genuinely believed in the case put forward at trial. The jury's role in deciding the genuineness of the police's belief creates a complication in malicious prosecution cases where the plaintiff claims that malice can be inferred from the absence of reasonable and probable cause. For this purpose they should be allowed to form their own view of what is reasonable and should not be directed by the judge (despite the fact that the judge must ultimately rule on the question of reasonable and probable cause himself after the jury has made its findings).[26]

In general, judges are reluctant to put a long list of specific questions to the jury because this may seem confusing. However, there are two obvious advantages in formulating specific questions to the jury.

First, if the jury are required to answer a compendious question, this will create complications because different jurors may arrive at the same conclusion by different routes. For example, if the jury is simply asked whether they find the police had reasonable grounds to believe that the plaintiff was committing a breach of the peace in a case where the plaintiff's and the police's version of events sharply conflicts, some jurors may find there were reasonable grounds by believing the police while others believe a mixture of the two versions.

Second, this practice also has the effect of the jury encroaching into the judge's function by deciding reasonable and probable

---

[26] *Hicks* v *Faulkner* [1878] 8 QBD 167, 175.

cause themselves. In order for the judge to make a ruling on this issue, it is necessary for the jury's answers to provide the detailed factual basis for that ruling.

How the jury should deal with damages

Two questions arise about how the jury should consider damages when making their assessment. First, there may be issues about the form of the question they should be asked. Second, practice differs about whether the jury should assess damages at the same time as they decide the questions on liability or whether they should be asked to retire a second time.

Some judges favour asking the jury to make a single award for damages whereas others ask the jury to specify any award they make for special damages[27] or exemplary damages.[28] The better approach is that the jury should spell out any award for special damages they give but that they should not make a separate award for exemplary damages.[29]

Another source of difficulty is whether the jury should decide the assessment of damages at the same time as the questions on liability or afterwards. Unless there are very few disputes of fact so that the jury's determination dispenses with any need for the judge to rule on reasonable and probable cause, it is necessary that the jury be sent out a second time to assess damages once the ruling has been made.

Closing speeches

After the judge is satisfied about the form of the questions to be put to the jury, the advocate for the police will give a closing speech. The advocate for the plaintiff will then follow.

No special principles apply to closing speeches although it is sensible to relate the arguments deployed to the questions the jury

---

[27]See p 39.
[28]See p 42.
[29]See *Cassell & Co* v *Broome* [1972] AC 1027, 1072, HL.

will be asked to answer. The jury should have copies of the questions available while the closing speeches are being made. In most police cases there are a limited number of jury questions and, as a result, closing speeches are often relatively short.

Previously, it was a clear rule of law that neither counsel nor the trial judge were permitted to mention figures to the jury. Thus, in a case where the plaintiff's counsel told the jury that the plaintiff's claim was, on the pleadings, limited to £50,000 the Court of Appeal held that the judge had been correct to discharge the jury and order a new trial.[30] However, since the decision in *Thompson*[31] it has become the practice for advocates to make reference to figures in closing speeches. The suggested level of damages will obviously begin with the "bracket" which the judge has decided on after hearing submissions in the absence of the jury. On the one hand, the advocate for the defendant will concentrate on "mitigating factors" such as the plaintiff's bad character or misconduct, tending to reduce the damages towards the bottom of the bracket. On the other hand, the advocate for the plaintiff will address the jury on the "aggravating" factors of the case, such as the conduct of the police officers and of the defence to the action. Strictly speaking, the figures mentioned by the advocates need not be limited to figures within the "bracket" because this is only for "guidance" and the jury is not bound to arrive at a damages figure within it. Nevertheless, a prudent advocate is unlikely to suggest a figure greatly above or below the bracket as this will bring him or her into conflict with the judge who will direct the jury on the basis of the bracket. If the jury follows an advocate and makes an award of damages substantially above or below the bracket, this is likely to lead to an award of damages which is overturned on appeal.

The judge's summing-up

The judge sums up to the jury on the relevant law and on the evidence. Summing up to juries should follow the conventional

---

[30] *Cole* v *Chief Constable of Merseyside*, 11 March 1993, unreported, CA.
[31] [1997] 2 All ER 774.
[32] *The Times*, 30 January 1996, CA.

pattern of summing up in criminal trials and the process of justice will be improved if the judge, in all but the very shortest cases, reminds the jury of the evidence and relates that evidence to the issues. Furthermore the judge's discretion to comment should only be used where the judge thinks it necessary in the interests of fairness.[33-34]

An appeal will lie if the judge gives a misdirection (such as misdirecting on the burden of proof) or if he misrepresents the evidence. However, for the purposes of making an appeal, the point should be taken before the trial judge. Consequently, if the judge has made some kind of misdirection, the objection should be taken in the absence of the jury at the end of the summing-up in order that it be rectified.

In the County Court it may avoid difficulties about keeping a proper note of the judge's summing-up if the advocates seek his permission to tape what is said.

The jury's verdict

The jury must give a unanimous verdict unless the judge rules that they have had a reasonable period to make a deliberation having regard to the nature and complexity of the case. The judge can then seek a majority verdict of 11–1 or 10–2 in the High Court, or 7–1 in the County Court. However, the parties themselves can accept a differently constituted majority verdict (such as 5–3) or the verdict of an incomplete jury (see generally section 17 of the Juries Act 1974).

In the course of arriving at a verdict the jury will often wish to ask the judge questions. The judge will hear argument from the advocates and, if necessary, make a ruling before calling the jury back to court and answering their query.

The judge's ruling on liability

Once the jury have returned their verdict, the judge will normally give a ruling on whether the police had reasonable cause for an

---

[33-34]See *Foster* v *Metropolitan Police Commissioner*, 17 October 1995, unreported, CA.

arrest or lacked reasonable and probable cause for commencing a prosecution.

In cases where there is a direct conflict about what actually happened, no ruling by the judge will usually be necessary. Either the plaintiff or the police will have been believed so that there will be nothing requiring a ruling from the judge. Assuming that the plaintiff wins, the jury will simply be asked to assess damages. It will normally be necessary for the jury to retire to consider damages if the judge rules in the plaintiff's favour or if the plaintiff has succeeded in proving an assault. On the other hand, if the police have been successful, they will apply for their costs.

However, where the jury finds for the plaintiff on some issues and for the police on others, the position is much more complicated. The argument before the judge may be extensive.

2. PROCEDURE AT TRIALS BEFORE JUDGE ALONE

The procedure followed in a judge-only trial brought against police is no different from that in an ordinary civil trial. The complications created by the different functions of the judge and jury in a jury trial do not come into play.

It is worth re-emphasising the discussion above (see p 117) in respect of the right to open the case. The plaintiff's advocate should open if damages are claimed which he must prove.[35] Therefore, even where the burden of proof in respect of all the issues on the pleadings lies on the defendant, for example where the only issue at trial is wrongful arrest, the plaintiff's advocate should still begin.

3. INTEREST AND COSTS

Interest

If interest is claimed, it must be pleaded.[36] Interest is available in the following circumstances:

---

[35] *Chapman* v *Rawson* [1846] 8 QB 673.
[36] RSC Ord 18 r 8; CCR Ord 5 r 1A.

- interest for pain and suffering in personal injury cases is awarded at 2% from the service of proceedings in all other cases no interest is awarded on general damages for non-economic loss such as damages for pain and suffering in false imprisonment.[37]
- interest is awarded on special damages at half the average rate of interest allowed under the Short Term Investment Account prevailing from the date they were incurred to trial;
- no interest is available on damages for any future loss of earnings or earning capacity.

Costs

Costs will usually follow the event so that the plaintiff will recover costs if he succeeds on any part of his claim. By the same token the defendant will be entitled to costs if the plaintiff fails. If, however, the plaintiff fails to recover the amount paid into court, the police will probably be able to obtain their costs from the date the payment was made.

Nevertheless, the question of costs is a matter of the judge's discretion. The successful party may be deprived of his costs if he presents a false case or acts oppressively in the action.[38] Consequently, the judge may take these factors into account as was done in the case of *Wilson & Farbridge* v *Metropolitan Police Commissioner*[39] where Tudor Price J refused to award costs to the police when the plaintiff failed to beat the payment into court and said:

> "the jury were of the opinion, on the balance of probabilities . . . that the case put forward by the Defendant in this Court was an untrue one supported by untrue evidence. In those circumstances, it seems to me, on further consideration to be quite wrong to order Mr Wilson to pay any part of the Defence's costs. . . . In my view, Mr Wilson was entitled to be vindicated by the jury's verdict and to have a jury express the view, as they undoubtedly have done, that the

---

[37] *Holtham* v *Metropolitan Police Commissioner, The Times*, 28 November 1987.
[38] *Baylis Baxter* v *Sabath* [1958] 1 WLR 529, CA.
[39] December 10 1985, unreported.

conduct of the individual police officers towards him was oppressive and abusive of their powers, and on reconsideration, therefore, I order that the costs of Mr Wilson should be paid by the Defendants."

The costs orders made in the County Court are that the plaintiff will recover scale costs on the following basis:

* exceeding £3,000, scale 2;
* exceeding £100 and not exceeding £3,000, scale 1;
* exceeding £25 and not exceeding £100, lower scale.

However, the trial judge has a discretion to award costs on such scale as he thinks fit if he certifies that there is a difficult question of law or a question of fact of exceptional complexity is involved (see CCR Order 38 rule 4(6)). The judge also has a discretion to award costs in an appropriate case on a lower scale than would otherwise apply.[40] This existence of this overriding discretion was confirmed by the Court of Appeal in the case of *Brown* v *Commissioner of Police of the Metropolis.*[41]

The exercise of a judge's discretion as to costs in a High Court action was considered in *Hewitt* v *Anderton*[42] The plaintiff had commenced an action in the High Court against the police. During the course of the action the plaintiff abandoned some of his claims and he was awarded £200 by the jury. The judge decided to award the plaintiff his costs on the High Court basis because the plaintiff was entitled to take the view that the jury ought to award him more than £5,000 (the limit of the County Court jurisdiction at that time) and because the case involved exposing significant police wrongdoing. The Court of Appeal refused to interfere with the judge's exercise of his discretion. In practice most cases issued in the High Court will now be transferred to the County Court. For those that remain in the High Court, the High Court no longer has the power to limit the costs awarded to the County Court scale (see Courts and Legal Services Act 1990, Schedule 20, which repealed section 19 of the County Courts Act 1984).

---

[40]CCR Ord 38 r 1(2); *Bourne* v *Stanbridge* [1965] 1 WLR 189, CA.
[41]*The Times*, 24 April 1996, CA.
[42]8 October 1991, unreported, CA.

4. APPEALS ARISING FROM JURY TRIALS

Introduction

The judiciary has traditionally been extremely reluctant to interfere with the verdicts of juries. They are chary of substituting their views for the conclusions of the jury and the grounds for making an appeal are therefore rather limited. The County Courts Appeal Order 1991 contains provisions for seeking leave to appeal in cases decided in the County Court. Where a plaintiff recovers less than £5,000 in a civil action against the police, he will now need to have leave before commencing an appeal.[43] If no damages have been awarded leave will also be required if the value of the claim is less than £5,000.[44] The value of the claim is "the amount which the plaintiff reasonably expects to recover" and is the same as that used when issues arise in respect of the transfer of cases between the High Court and the County Court.[45] Every notice of appeal from the County Court must be accompanied by a certificate of value.[46]

Appeals where an issue was incorrectly left to the jury

If it can be demonstrated that the trial judge erred in law in allowing the jury to make a determination when they should never have done so, then the procedure for an appeal is uncomplicated. No difficulties arise about the Court of Appeal substituting its views for the jury since the jury should not have reached a conclusion in the first place. An example of an appeal on this ground can be found in the case of *Middleweek* v *Chief Constable of Merseyside*[47] in which the Court of Appeal held that the trial judge had wrongly left the issue of false imprisonment to the jury. The defendant's appeal was upheld and the jury's award of damages was overturned.

Appeals are therefore straightforward if the judge makes an error of law such as allowing the jury to give a verdict on malice in a

---

[43]County Courts Appeal Order 1991 (SI 1991 No 1877), art 2(1)(a)(i).
[44]*Ibid*, art 2(6).
[45]See p 133 above.
[46]RSC Ord 59, r 3A.
[47][1992] 1 AC 179, CA.

malicious prosecution case when there is no evidence to put before it or where the jury makes an assessment of damages after the judge has incorrectly ruled that the police were guilty of a wrongful arrest. For the appeal to succeed all that must be shown is that the judge has made a mistake of law.

Appeals where an issue was properly left to the jury

If, however, it is accepted that it was correct for an issue to have been left for determination by the jury, it is necessary to persuade the Court of Appeal to order a new trial under RSC Order 59 rule 11.

The Court of Appeal will not make such an order unless it can be shown that some substantial wrong or miscarriage has been caused and that one of the following grounds for an appeal exists:[48]

- there has been a misdirection;
- evidence at the trial was improperly admitted or rejected;
- the verdict of the jury was not taken on an issue which the trial judge was not asked to put to them.

However, an appeal may be made concerning only some of the various issues decided at trial.[49] For example, the Court of Appeal could order a new trial solely on the issue of false imprisonment or on the question of whether exemplary damages should have been awarded.

If the Court of Appeal orders a new trial, the issues decided and rulings given at the first trial are not *res judicata* and are not binding at the re-trial which is a trial *de novo*.[50]

The most common grounds for instituting an appeal are:

- A misdirection by the judge in his summing-up. This includes a positive misdirection such as stating the burden of proof incorrectly or failing to direct the jury on an issue which they should have been directed on. Normally, a new trial will not be granted unless the point was raised at trial.[51]

---

[48]RSC Ord 59 r 11(2).
[49]RSC Ord 59 r 11(3).
[50]*Bobolas* v *Economist Newspaper* [1987] 1 WLR 1101; [1987] 3 All ER 12, CA.
[51]*Nevill* v *Fine Art and General Insurance* [1897] AC 68, 76.

- The improper admission or rejection of evidence is a ground for a new trial. The appeal will not succeed if the evidence could not have had a legitimate effect on the verdict[52] or if the objection was not taken at trial and could have been dealt with by calling other evidence.[53]
- Improperly withdrawing the case from the jury will entitle the plaintiff to a new trial; this would be appropriate where the judge incorrectly removes a case from the jury and nonsuits the plaintiff.[54]
- Misleading the jury such as leaving them a question which is in fact a question for the trial judge.[55]
- A perverse verdict is given: in practice, such an appeal will be very difficult to pursue because it must be demonstrated that no reasonable jury properly directed could have come to the verdict on the evidence; if reasonable men might have found that verdict, the appeal will fail.[56]
- Misconduct of the jury generally, for example, if a stranger was in the jury room for a substantial period while the jury were considering their verdict.[57]
- New fresh evidence: applications for leave to adduce further evidence will only succeed in certain specified and exceptional circumstances.[58] Where the trial was in the County Court, the application for a new trial should be made to the County Court judge.[59] The Court of Appeal will be slow to allow an appeal because of new evidence. This was demonstrated in the case of *Lawrence* v *Metropolitan Police Commissioner*[60] when the Court of Appeal refused to allow new evidence to be admitted despite the fact that, if accepted as true, the evidence would show that the plaintiff had lied and that there was no assault or malicious prosecution. The fresh evidence was the testimony of a witness who had been a prosecution witness in the criminal prosecution,

---

[52]*Manley* v *Palache* [1895] 73 LT 98.
[53]*Bradshaw* v Widdrington [1902] 2 Ch 430, 449.
[54]*Brearley* v *LNWR* (1899) 15 TLR 237.
[55]*Abrahams* v *Dimmock* [1915] 1 KB 662, CA.
[56]*Metropolitan Railway* v *Wright* [1886] 11 App Cas 152, 156.
[57]*Goby* v *Wetherill* [1915] 2 KB 674.
[58]See *Supreme Court Practice 1997* (Sweet and Maxwell) notes to Ord 59 r 10 at 59/10/7 and notes to RSC Ord 59 r 19 at 59/19/12.
[59]CCR Ord 37 r 1.
[60]15 February 1991, unreported.

in which he now said he had lied. The majority of the court found no credible reason, such as coercion or bribery, for why he had lied to the Crown Court on two previous occasions, and as such, did not believe that he could be trusted to tell the truth on this occasion.

Appeals on assessments of damages

By RSC Order 59 rule 11(4)

"In any case where the Court of Appeal has power to order a new trial on the ground that damages awarded by a jury are excessive or inadequate, the Court may, instead of ordering a new trial substitute for the sum awarded by the jury such sum as appears to the court to be proper."

This rule applies to appeals set down on or after 1 February 1991. The circumstances in which a new trial can be ordered are illustrated by *Storey* v *Chief Constable of Lancashire*.[61] The plaintiff had been awarded £5,000 compensatory damages for being dragged down approximately 30 steps and along a pavement for about 40 yards to a police van and then forcefully shoved inside it. The Court of Appeal, applied the following test:

"are the damages so excessive that no twelve men could reasonably have given them, or perhaps more appropriately, there must be some reasonable relation between the wrong done and the solatium applied".

The Court of Appeal took the view that the award of £5,000 was out of all proportion to the injury suffered and remitted the case for a new trial. However, the Court of Appeal will now assess damages themselves and will apply a stricter test when considering the appropriateness of the award. Thus, in *Lewis* v *Chief Constable of Greater Manchester*[62] the Court of Appeal assessed the damages themselves. The plaintiff was wrongfully arrested and kept in bedclothes at the police station for 62 hours. The jury awarded

[61] 28 January 1991, unreported.
[62] *The Independent*, 23 October 1991.

£17,500 compensatory damages. The Court of Appeal took the view that no reasonable jury could properly make such an award. Parker LJ pointed out that it represented a rate of over £250,00 per month or about £3 million a year. The Court of Appeal assessed the damages at £5,000. The Court of Appeal in *Thompson*[62a] made it clear that it would not hesitate to review damages awards by juries which were too high or too low.

5. APPEALS IN JUDGE ONLY TRIALS

Introduction

No special principles apply to appeals made in police cases where the trial was decided by a judge only. An appeal will succeed if it can be shown that the judge has erred on the usual conventional grounds.

Appeals on liability

After a trial before a judge sitting without a jury, the judge makes an order which can then be subject to appeal. An appeal is available if the judge makes an error of law and may be made against the judge's decisions of fact and against the wrongful exercise of a discretion.

If a judge is wrong in law, the Court of Appeal can correct him and no special principles apply. The prospect of successfully appealing against the trial judge on other grounds which are potentially available is not high. If an appeal is sought against the judge's determination of fact, the Court of Appeal will place great weight on the fact that first instance judge had the opportunity to evaluate the witnesses and form a view about their credit. On the other hand, if an appeal is made against the judge's exercise of a discretion, it must be shown that it is plainly wrong.

[62a][1997] 2 All ER 774.

138

Appealing a judge's award of damages

If damages at trial can be challenged because the judge made an error of law (by, for example, applying the wrong test of remoteness), the Court of Appeal will simply correct the determination. However, where the assessment of damages itself is under appeal, the Court of Appeal will only interfere if the judge must have acted upon some wrong principle of law or is such an "entirely erroneous estimate of the damage" as to be perverse.[63] The Court of Appeal will not, therefore, interfere if the judge's award of damages falls within an appropriate range.

---

[63] *Flint* v *Lovell* [1935] 1 KB 354 at 360.

Contents of Chapter 7

Chapter 7
Precedents

1. INTRODUCTION

The precedents are based on a fictitious incident as follows:

"On 21 January 1996 in the early morning, Mr Stuart Locke was walking along Quinton Street, Gotham when he was stopped by PC Berkeley and PC Hume of the Barsetshire police and asked questions about his whereabouts that evening. Mr Locke refused to answer any questions and walked away. At this point PC Hume seized Mr Locke's arm and forcibly restrained him from leaving. A fracas then took place in the course of which Mr Locke was struck on the face and body. His jacket and watch were damaged.

The two police officers then bundled Mr Locke into a police car which conveyed him to Ulmthorpe Police Station. A custody record was opened which recorded the reason for his arrest as 'obstructing a police officer in the execution of his duty'. His detention was authorised by the custody officer 'to obtain evidence by questioning'. Mr Locke asked to see his solicitor but this was refused.

Mr Locke was charged with being drunk and disorderly and obstructing a police officer in the execution of his duty. The charged were dismissed by the magistrates after a trial on 15 October 1996. As a result of being charged and tried Mr Locke lost earnings of £400 and incurred legal costs of £250."

2. **LETTER BEFORE ACTION**

Dear Sir

Re: Stuart Locke

We act for the above-named, who was arrested on 21 January 1996 and subsequently charged with the offences of being drunk and disorderly and assaulting a police officer in the execution of his duty. As you are aware, the charges were dismissed by the Gotham Magistrates Court on 15 October 1996. Mr Locke was arrested after being stopped in the street at approximately 5am.

He was seized by the arm by a police officer and then struck a number of times in the course of a purported arrest.

As you are well aware, the burden of justifying this arrest, and Mr Locke's subsequent detention, is on the Chief Constable. On our instructions there was no material before the arresting officers capable of providing such justification. If this is correct, it would follow that Mr Locke has a good cause of action against the Chief Constable for wrongful arrest and false imprisonment.

We are also instructed that the written statements and the evidence upon which our client's prosecution was based were fabricated and false, and that the prosecution was instituted and continued without reasonable and probable cause and maliciously. In summary, we have advised our client that he was assaulted, wrongfully arrested and maliciously prosecuted.

Unless we receive, within 28 days, information satisfactory to our client to justify his arrest and detention or proposals satisfactory to our client for compensation we are instructed to serve proceedings on the Chief Constable for damages, including aggravated and exemplary damages, without further notice.

Our client has also instructed us to make a complaint on his behalf in relation to these matters under Part IX of the Police and Criminal Evidence Act 1984. A formal authority in writing is enclosed.

Yours faithfully,

J. Bentham & Co (Solicitors)

3. PARTICULARS OF CLAIM

IN THE GOTHAM COUNTY COURT   *Case No.*

BETWEEN:

STUART LOCKE   *Plaintiff*

- and -

THE CHIEF CONSTABLE OF
THE BARSETSHIRE POLICE   *Defendant*

PARTICULARS OF CLAIM

---

1. The Defendant is and was at all material times the Chief Officer
   of Police for the Barsetshire police area and the police officers
   hereinafter referred to were at all material times acting under
   his direction and control in the performance or purported performance of their police functions within the meaning of the
   Police Act 1964.
2. On 21 January 1996, at about 5am, the Plaintiff was walking
   along Quinton Street, Gotham when he was assaulted by police officers who seized him by the arm and then assaulted and
   beat him by striking him on the face and arms.
3. The Plaintiff was then wrongfully arrested by the said police
   officers.
4. Following his said wrongful arrest, the Plaintiff was taken to
   Ulmthorpe Police Station where his detention was purportedly
   authorised at 5.41am, "in order to obtain evidence by questioning". The Plaintiff was not in fact questioned until 4.15pm
   on 21 January 1996.
5. The said arrest and detention were unlawful, not being
   founded upon reasonable suspicion of the commission by the
   Plaintiff of an arrestable offence, or other lawful authority.
6. Further or alternatively, the said arrest was unlawful in that the
   Plaintiff was not informed of the reason for his arrest.

Police Actions

7. If, which is denied, the said arrest was lawful, the Plaintiff was held in police custody for an unreasonably long period.

8. The Plaintiff was prosecuted by police officers for being drunk and disorderly and assaulting a police officer in the execution of his duty. The said prosecution terminated in the Plaintiff's favour on 15 October 1996 when the charges were dismissed.

9. At about 7pm on 21 January 1996 the Plaintiff was released on police bail, having been unlawfully detained for about 14 hours.

10. The said prosecution of the Plaintiff was instituted and continued by police officers maliciously and without reasonable or probable cause.

PARTICULARS

(a) At a time unknown to the Plaintiff but prior to his being charged the said police officers fabricated a false account of the events giving rise to his arrest, in that they falsely alleged that the Plaintiff had smelt of alcohol, had been abusive towards them, and had struck the arresting officer.

(b) The said police officers knew that the account they gave was false. They knew that there were no reasonable grounds for suspecting that the Plaintiff had committed any offence and that consequently they had no grounds for bringing any prosecution against the Plaintiff and that such prosecution lacked reasonable and probable cause.

The Plaintiff will rely on the matters aforesaid as evidence of malice.

11. By reason of the matters aforesaid, the Plaintiff suffered loss, damage, distress, anxiety, humiliation, damage to his reputation, and was deprived of his liberty.

PARTICULARS OF INJURIES

(a) Bruising to the right arm;
(b) Bruising to the face;
(c) Cuts to the face;
(d) Severe bruising to the rib cage;

(e) As a result of the said bruises, the Plaintiff had difficulties in sleeping for a period of about a week. The Plaintiff will rely on the report of Dr Jekyll dated 30 October 1996.

PARTICULARS OF SPECIAL DAMAGE

Damage to the Plaintiff's jacket	£45.00
Loss of earnings	£400.00
Legal Costs	£250.00

12. Further, by reason of the matters aforesaid the Plaintiff is entitled to aggravated damages.
13. Further, the actions of the said police officers were arbitrary, oppressive and unconstitutional and the Plaintiff claims exemplary damages.
14. Further, the Plaintiff claims interest pursuant to section 69 of the County Courts Act 1984 on such sums as are found due to the Plaintiff at such rate and for such period as the Court thinks fit.

AND the Plaintiff claims:

(1) Damages, including aggravated and exemplary damages, in excess of £5,000;
(2) The aforesaid interest pursuant to section 35A of the Supreme Court Act 1981, to be assessed.

PETER HARE

Dated, etc

4. DEFENCE

IN THE GOTHAM COUNTY COURT   *Case No.*

BETWEEN:

STUART LOCKE   *Plaintiff*

- and -

THE CHIEF CONSTABLE OF
THE BARSETSHIRE POLICE   *Defendant*

DEFENCE

---

1. The Defendant admits paragraph 1 of the Particulars of Claim.
2. It is admitted and averred that at about 5am on 21 January 1996 the Plaintiff was lawfully arrested by PC Berkeley who reasonably suspected him of being in the process of committing the offences of being drunk and disorderly contrary to section 91(1) of the Criminal Justice Act 1967 and assaulting a police officer in the execution of his duty.

PARTICULARS

(a) PC Berkeley and PC Hume, acting on information received, approached the Plaintiff in Quinton Road, Gotham from the said junction.

(b) The said police officers stopped the Plaintiff and asked his name and address but the Plaintiff refused to answer any questions.

(c) The said police officers repeated the questions but the Plaintiff again refused to answer any questions. The officers noticed that the Plaintiff's eyes were glazed, his breath smelt of intoxicating liquor and he was unsteady on his feet. He had in his hand a can of Carlsberg "Special Brew". The officers formed the view that he was drunk.

(d) The Plaintiff began to shout, became aggressive and abusive and punched PC Hume on the arm as he began to move away whereupon PC Berkeley seized the Plaintiff's arm, arrested him and advised him that he was being arrested on the ground that he was obstructing the police in the execution of their duty.

(e) A struggle then took place between the officers PC Berkeley and PC Hume and the Plaintiff in which the said police officers used reasonable force to subdue the Plaintiff.

3. In the premises, it is averred that PC Berkeley used as much force as was reasonable to arrest the Plaintiff.

4. Save as aforesaid, paragraphs 2 and 3 of the Particulars of Claim are denied.

5. Paragraph 4 of the Particulars of Claim is admitted. The Defendant had reasonable grounds for detaining the Plaintiff to obtain evidence by questioning him in relation to the offence for which he had been arrested.

6. It is accordingly denied that the Plaintiff's detention was unlawful. Save as aforesaid, paragraphs 5 to 7 of the Statement of Claim are admitted.

7. It is denied that the Plaintiff was prosecuted maliciously and without reasonable and probable cause and the Defendant will rely upon the matters referred to in paragraph 2 hereof.

8. The Defendant denies the Plaintiff has suffered loss and damage as alleged or at all or that he is entitled to exemplary damages, aggravated damages or interest as claimed or at all. Further the Defendant avers that if, which is not admitted, the Plaintiff suffered any injury, that the Plaintiff was the author of his own misfortune, by unlawfully resisting his lawful arrest.

HENRY BERGSON

Served etc.

5. REQUEST FOR FURTHER AND BETTER PARTICULARS OF THE DEFENCE

IN THE GOTHAM COUNTY COURT   *Case No.*

BETWEEN:

STUART LOCKE   ***Plaintiff***

- and -

THE CHIEF CONSTABLE OF
THE BARSETSHIRE POLICE   ***Defendant***

REQUEST FOR FURTHER AND BETTER
PARTICULARS OF THE DEFENCE

Under Paragraph 2
1. Of ". . . the Plaintiff was lawfully arrested by PC Berkeley who reasonably suspected him of being in the process of committing the offences of being drunk and disorderly . . .".

(i) State whether the Defendant intends, at trial, to rely on any facts or matters in addition to those already pleaded as justifying the alleged arrest;
(ii) If so, give full particulars of the same.

Under Paragraph 2: Particulars
2. Of: "(a) PC Berkeley and PC Hume, acting on information received . . ."
State the nature of the information received, the source of the information, and when it was received.

3. Of: "(d) The Plaintiff began to shout, became aggressive and abusive and punched PC Hume on the arm . . ."
(i) State what it is alleged that the Plaintiff did or said when he allegedly became aggressive and abusive;
(ii) State the nature of the punch it is alleged that the Plaintiff threw;

(iii) Specify where it is alleged that he struck PC Hume on the arm.

4. Of "(e) A struggle then took place between the officers PC Berkeley and PC Hume and the Plaintiff in which the said police officers used reasonable force to subdue the Plaintiff".
(i) Give full particulars of the struggle which is alleged to have taken place;
(ii) Specify all facts and matters relied on in support of the allegation that the force used by the said police officers was reasonable as alleged.

Under Paragraph 5
6. Of "the Defendant had reasonable grounds for detaining the Plaintiff".
(i) State whether the Defendant relies upon any facts or matters in addition to those pleaded in support of the allegation that the Plaintiff was lawfully detained;
(ii) If so, give full particulars of the same.

PETER HARE

Dated, etc

6. STATEMENT IN OPEN COURT

IN THE GOTHAM COUNTY COURT   *Case No.*

BETWEEN:

STUART LOCKE   *Plaintiff*

- and -

THE CHIEF CONSTABLE OF
THE BARSETSHIRE POLICE   *Defendant*

STATEMENT IN OPEN COURT

---

1. The Plaintiff in this action, Mr Stuart Locke, is now aged 22 years. At the time of the relevant events in January 1996, he was aged 19 years.
2. The Defendant is the Chief Constable for the Barsetshire Police, and is responsible in law for the police officers whose actions form the subject of Mr Locke's claim. Those officers, PC Berkeley and PC Hume, were based at Ulmthorpe police station.
3. The Plaintiff's claim against the Defendant is for damages for false imprisonment, assault and malicious prosecution. He claims that he was wrongfully arrested and unlawfully detained at Ulmthorpe police station, that he was assaulted and injured in the course of that wrongful arrest, and that he was prosecuted for criminal offences, of which he was innocent, on the basis of evidence fabricated by PC Berkeley and PC Hume. The Plaintiff claims aggravated damages to compensate him for the anxiety, distress and humiliation he suffered, and exemplary damages to reflect the arbitrary and unconstitutional nature of the police misconduct.
4. The events giving rise to this claim are as follows [see *Particulars of Claim*].
5. The Plaintiff has maintained from the start that PC Berkeley and PC Hume concocted and fabricated the allegations against him with the intention that he would be wrongfully convicted of

offences of which they knew him to be innocent. The Chief Constable has refused to apologise for or to acknowledge the alleged misconduct of his officers. Indeed, by his pleadings in this action, the Chief Constable has repeated the allegations made against Mr Locke. He continues to deny liability. Nevertheless, he has paid to Mr Locke the sum of £10,000.

Appendix 1
Questionnaire for the potential plaintiff

(1) How, where and when were you arrested? Give the full circumstances of the arrest in as much detail as possible, including the names/descriptions of the arresting officers involved.

(2) Were there witnesses to the arrest and, if so, what are their names and addresses?

(3) Were you told that you were under arrest? If so, when?

(4) Were you told the reason for the arrest? If so, when and in precisely what words?

(5) Were you handcuffed? If so, when, by whom and for how long?

(6) Was any property seized by the police? If so, what steps did the police take in seizing it?

(7) Was any property damaged and, if so, how and by which police officers? What is the cost of repairing any damage to property (attach copies of any receipts for their repair or replacement)?

(8) If the police entered your home or arrested you at home, did they have a warrant and what steps did they take.

(9) Did the police act abusively towards you? If so, who was abusive and what did they say and do?

(10) Were you searched when arrested and what steps did the police take?

(11) Were you held in custody at the police station? If so, for how long?

(12) What were you told was the reason for your detention?

(13) Were you given an opportunity to make representations when this detention was being reviewed?

(14) Were you interviewed? If so, by who, in what manner and what was said?

(15) What were the conditions of detention like? Were you provided with blankets and regular meals?

Police Actions

(16) Were you subjected to a strip search or intimate body search, or had a body sample taken while in custody? If so, give details. Were you told the reason for the search?

(17) Were you assaulted by police officers? If so, when, how and by which police officers?

(18) Did you complain of an assault? If you were seen by a police surgeon, were photographs taken.

(19) Were any costs incurred as a result of your arrest, detention or assault? For example, loss of earnings (net of tax), damage to clothing, cost of medical expenses. Please produce any documentary evidence.

(20) Do you have previous criminal convictions? If so, what are they? Have you spent time in prison or police custody?

(21) Were you prosecuted for any offence? If so, what were the charges, on which occasions did you have to go to court, what was the final outcome of the prosecution?

(22) Did your arrest or prosecution attract any publicity? If so, what publicity? (Attach copies of any newspaper articles).

(23) Did the prosecution put you livelihood in jeopardy? If so, please give details.

Appendix 2
Table of Damages Awards

1. ASSAULTs

Leon v Commr of Police for the Metropolis [1986] CLY 2538, Clerkenwell CC.	P was a 26-year-old Rastafarian. He stated that in July 1982 two police constables asked if they could search him for drugs. He explained that he had already been searched and ran to catch a bus. He was pursued, pulled off the bus platform and pushed against a fence. He was then punched, kicked and thrown into a police van. He claimed damages for swollen bruised lips, a swollen nose and forehead and bruises to his back. He suffered no lasting injuries. The police denied the assault and that any injuries had been sustained, alternatively they had been sustained as he resisted a lawful arrest. The court found that the degree of force used was excessive and unreasonable, that P had offered no violence but the officers had treated him as though he were a violent criminal. It was strongly suspected that the motive of the police was prejudice against a black man with an outlandish costume and strange accent.	Compensatory damages of £200. Exemplary damages of £1,000 to mark a flagrant abuse of the police's considerable powers (1996 value: £314, and £1,570 respectively).
Drake v Ministry of Defence (1988) Legal Action, 23 November, Westminster CC.	P was arrested at Greenham Common and placed in a police meals room where adverse comments were made and one officer slowly and deliberately poured a mug of hot coffee down her arm. She was twice thrown against a wall and suffered pain and redress to the arm for the evening and part of the following day and a slight bruise to the lower back.	Compensatory damages: £10 for arm, £75 for bruised back. Exemplary damages of £400 (1996 value £15; £110 and £590 respectively).

157

| *Dousett and Tape v Commr of Police of the Metropolis* [1989] CLY 1260. | P1 and P2 left a party at a wine bar with others in the early hours of the morning and started looking for a taxi. P2, who was drunk, flagged down a police car and in the course of conversation told a WPC "you talk common for a copper". P2's wife apologised and they continued on their way. Additional police vehicles soon arrived and after a brief exchange a police officer grabbed P2 round the neck and arrested him. When P1 protested he too was grabbed by the arms and arrested. At the police station, the WPC assaulted P2 by slapping him across the face while other officers held him by the arms and legs. P2 was assaulted causing him to black out and to sustain a double fracture of the mandible, bruising and lacerations necessitating surgery. He was taken to hospital. P2 was released about 4½ hours after his arrest. The police maintained that both plaintiffs had been drunk and disorderly and had assaulted police officers. Both P1 and P2 were acquitted of being drunk and disorderly and assaulting the police officers. | P1 was awarded the following: compensatory damages of £500 and exemplary damages of £800 for false imprisonment; £5,000 compensatory damages and £5,000 exemplary damages for assault; compensatory damages £5,000 and £10,000 exemplary damages for malicious prosecution. Total award £26,300 (1996 value: £35,768). P2 was awarded the following: compensatory damages of £100 and exemplary damages of £200 for false imprisonment; compensatory damages £500 and exemplary damages £5,000 for assault; compensatory damages £5,000 and exemplary damages £10,000 for malicious prosecution. Total award £20,800 (1996 value: £28,288). |

Case	Facts	Damages
Garfinkle v Commr of Police of the Metropolis [1989] CLY 1261, Bow CC, HHJ Burkett Baker without a jury.	P who had convictions for, *inter alia*, possession of cannabis was detained on the street by two police sergeants who, the court accepted, had reasonable grounds to suspect he was in possession of drugs. He refused to be searched so the police officers decided to take him to the police station to search him pursuant to s 23 of the Misuse of Drugs Act 1971. On the street and/or in the back of the police car he was punched in the mouth/nose, causing a puncture of the lower lip by a tooth and one or two external lacerations. The wounds healed in the course of a month leaving quite insignificant scars. After being searched with a negative result he was detained a further 50 minutes without lawful justification. He was released without charge and then complained to another police station.	The judge made a global award in respect of the the assault in the sum of £1,200 to include general, compensatory, aggravated damages plus special damages of £62.50. He awarded £250 for the false imprisonment. Total award £1,470 (1996 value: £2,000).
Spencer v Chief Constable of W Yorkshire (News report, *The Times*, 9 February 1990) Fennel J and jury.	P suffered a broken lip, damaged jaw and teeth.	Compensatory damages £750. Exemplary damages £5,000 (1996 value £950 and £6,350 respectively).
Riley v Chief Constable of W Yorkshire, (News report, *The Guardian*, 19 December 1990) HC, Morland J and jury.	P, who was a miner, was struck on the head and body by riot police. He was then knocked out with a truncheon blow and required 4 stiches. He was also held at the pit manager's office when he was again struck with a truncheon. He was later maliciously prosecuted for breach of the peace.	Compensatory damages: £4,000 (assault), £5,500 (false imprisonment) £500 (malicious prosecution). Exemplary damages: £50,000 (1996 value: £5,080, £6,985, £635 and £63,500 respectively).
Cusworth v Chief Constable of S Yorkshire (News report, *The Guardian*, 10 July 1991) May J and jury.	P, a road sweeper, was attacked by police in riot gear during a miner's strike. He was dragged over his garden and kicked in the neck and shoulder until he blacked out. He was then detained in custody.	Compensatory and exemplary damages: £60,000 (1996 value: £69,600).

Case	Facts	Damages
Burke v *Met Police Commr*, Croydon CC, with a jury (News report, *The Times*, 20 March 1992)	P was pulled to the ground and held down by 3 police officers after trying to give her disabled husband a diabetes tablet. She was unlawfully arrested and maliciously prosecuted for assaulting police.	£20,000 for assault, £15,000 for false imprisonment and £15,000 for malicious prosecution were awarded (1996 value £22,400; £16,800 and £16,800 respectively).
Barnes v *Commr of Police for the Metropolis* [1992] CLY 1781, Croydon CC with a jury.	P was wrongfully arrested in 1985 and held in police custody for 4 hours. Whilst in custody he was assaulted by one or more police officers on one or two occasions. The most serious assault involved P being struck with an implement, probably a truncheon, causing a double fracture to the clavicle. He was left with a bony prominence, but no real functional disability or long-term effects. Further surgery to remove the prominence was ruled out.	Compensatory and aggravated damages in the sum of £2,500 (1966 value: £2,800) were awarded for false imprisonment and no exemplary damages. Compensatory and aggravated damages of £10,000 were awarded for the assault (1996 value: £11,200) with a further £10,000 awarded for exemplary damages.
Connor v *Chief Constable of Cambridgeshire*, *The Times*, 11 April 1994, HC, French J.	P was struck over the head with a truncheon at a football match.	Compensatory damages £2,000; exemplary damages of £500 (1996 value: £2,140 and £535 respectively).
Sturley v *Met Police Commr*, *The Times*, 27 June 1994.	P's arm was twisted and fractured in the course of a lawful arrest.	Damages £2,000 (1996 value: £2,140).

160

Case	Facts	Damages
Treadaway v *Chief Constable of W Midlands The Independent*, 23 September 1994; *The Times*, 25 October 1994, McKinnon J.	P, who had a serious criminal record was seriously assaulted and "tortured" by police officers in order to obtain a confession. As a result, he was subsequently convicted of armed robbery.	Compensatory damages £2,500; aggravated damages £7,500; exemplary damages £40,000 (1996 values £2,675, £8,025 and £42,800 respectively).
Forde v *Home Office* [1994] CLY 1479.	P was assaulted by other prisoners as a result of prison officer's negligence.	£750 for the first assault and £1,000 for the second assault (1996 values £800 and £1,070).
Hulley v *Met Police Commr*, 14 December 1995, unreported, Central London CC with a jury.	P, who was of good character, attended a stag party together with a friend. In the early hours of the morning P was whistling a Laurel and Hardy tune which police officers objected to. An altercation ensued which resulted in P being bruised and cut around the face. Police officers involved alleged that P had fallen over a wall. He was detained for about 6 hours. He was prosecuted under s 5 of the Public Order Act 1986 but acquitted after trial in the Magistrates' Court.	Compensatory damages for unlawful arrest and false imprisonment, assault and malicious prosecution were awarded in the sum of £16,500.
Martyn Bryan v *Met Police Commr*, 13 March 1996, unreported, Central London CC with a jury.	P, who was black and of good character was stopped by police officers whilst driving his Peugeot 205 car. They alleged that he was driving dangerously. When P went to his car to get his Filofax in order to write down the identification numbers of the police officers he was arrested, placed in handcuffs and put in a police van. Whilst in the van his arms were swung in such a way that he sustained soft tissue injuries. His arms remained in a light cast for 6 weeks. After being detained about 2 hours he was prosecuted under s 5 of the Public Order Act 1986. At trial he alleged that he had only been stopped by the police officers because he was black.	Compensatory damages of £7,500 were awarded for unlawful arrest, assault and malicious prosecution. Exemplary damages £20,000.

Case	Facts	Award
Goswell v Met Police Commr (News report, *The Guardian*, 27 April 1996).	P was handcuffed to police officers and then struck on the head with a truncheon causing a wound requiring 5 stitches and leaving a permanent scar. He was arrested and charged with assault on the police and threatening behaviour. During the trial the police officer involved in the assault stated that he did not regret his behaviour.	£120,000 for the assault; £12,000 for false imprisonment; £170,000 exemplary damages. It is understood the award is being appealed.
Woods v Chief Constable of Nottinghamshire [1996] 4 CL 213.	P, who was 18, suffered an assault by a police officer causing pain and discomfort for 1 week. He was wrongfully arrested for threatening behaviour and falsely imprisoned for about 3 hours. He was prosecuted under s 4 of the Public Order Act 1986 and acquitted 2 months later. The police pursued allegations of P's guilt in civil proceedings.	Damages: £5,000. Exemplary damages £45,000.
Hsu v Met Police Commr (News report, *The Times*, 29 March 1996) Central London CC with a jury.	P, a hairdresser, was unlawfully arrested after refusing to allow officers into his home without a warrant. His arms were twisted behind his back and he was handcuffed. He was then punched and kicked in the kidneys in the police van. His back was used as a footstool and he was racially abused. He was released at 11pm wearing only jeans and flip-flops. When he arrived home, he found that the door had been left open by the police and that his stereo and other property had been stolen. Upon examination by a doctor he was found to have extensive bruising to his back and kidneys.	Damages: £220,000. It is understood that the Commissioner is appealing against the size of the award.
Bozkurt & Ates v Commr of Police Central London CC with a jury (News report, *The Times*, 14 June 1996).	Two Turkish Kurds who have lived in Britain since 1989 were awarded damages for false imprisonment, malicious prosecution and assault. The men were punched after they were arrested for violent disorder during a protest in North London. One of them was hit with a truncheon. They were charged with violent disorder.	Mr Bozkurt was awarded compensatory damages of £18,200 and £55,000 exemplary damages. Mr Ates was awarded £22,000 compensatory and £55,000 exemplary damages. A stay in respect of all but £35,000 per plaintiff was obtained by the defendant who will consider whether to appeal.

| Gerald v Commr of Police, Central London CC (News report, The Times, 19 July 1996). | P was a telecommunications engineer from Hayes. He had been trying to get more police in his district to combat drug problems and was assaulted after being arrested during an anti-drugs operation on the Mozart estate in Queen's Park where he lived in 1990. He had written to his MP expressing his concern at drug problems. He was put in a headlock in the back of a van by four police officers and repeatedly punched. Officers hit him in the eyes, making blood vessels burst. He was dragged into the police station and strip searched. He was convicted of assaulting 2 officers but in May 1991 the conviction was overturned on appeal. | Compensatory and aggravated damages of £25,000 for assault, false imprisonment and malicious prosecution and exemplary damages of £100,000. |

2. FALSE IMPRISONMENT

(In the following cases the Court of Appeal has approved or substituted the damages award made)

Wershof v Metropolitan Police Commissioner [1978] 3 All ER 540.	P was a newly qualified solicitor who refused to hand a ring over to the police so they arrested him for obstructing them in the execution of their duty. He was detained for just over an hour.	Compensatory damages of £1,000 (1996 value £3,150).
Reynolds v Commissioner of Police of the Metropolis [1985] QB 881, CA, Caulfield J and a jury.	P was wrongfully arrested because of an unreasonable suspicion that she was involved with her co-habitee in criminal activity. She was detained for 14 hours.	Compensatory damages: £12,000 (1996 value: £25,920). The Court of Appeal rejected the Commissioner's appeal against quantum ([1982] Crim LR 600).
Ward v Chief Constable of Somerset & Avon Constabulary, The Times, 17 July 1985. Appeal on damages.	P was arrested on suspicion of theft and kept in custody unnecessarily long for 2½ hours.	Compensatory damages: £750 (1996 value: £1,245).
Houghton v Chief Constable of Greater Manchester (1987) 84 Cr App R 319, CA.	P was wrongfully arrested for having an offensive weapon and detained for 2½ hours.	CA assessed compensatory damages at £600 (1996 value: £910).

Case	Facts	Damages
Castorina v *Chief Constable of Surrey* (1988) NLJ 180 (CA reversing the judge's ruling on the lawfulness of the arrest).	The police arrested P, who was of good character, at home for theft from her former employer and detained her for 3¾ hours.	Damages: £4,500 (1996 value: £6,615).
Lewis v *Chief Constable of Greater Manchester, The Independent*, 23 October 1991.	P was wrongully arrested and kept in bedclothes at the police station for 62 hours.	The HC jury awarded compensatory damages of £2,500 for wrongful arrest and £17,500 for wrongful detention. The award was reduced on appeal to £2,500 for the wrongful arrest and £5,000 for the wrongful detention (1996 value: £2,900 and £5,800 respectively).
Lunt v *Liverpool City Justices*, 5 May 1991, unreported.	P was unlawfully imprisoned for rates arrears for a period of 6 weeks.	A Master assessed damages at £13,000. On appeal, the CA increased the damages to £25,000 (1996 value: £29,000).
Shah v *Commr of Police*, 17 October 1991, unreported.	P was punched in the course of a wrongful arrest and then detained for 3 hours 10 minutes.	CA awarded compensatory damages of £500 for the assault, £300 for false imprisonment and £700 exemplary damages (1996 value: £580, £350 and £810 respectively).

Case	Facts	Damages
Cumber v Chief Constable of Hampshire Constabulary [1995] CLY 159.	A 15-year-old girl was wrongly detained in police custody for 4½ hours.	Exemplary damages of £50 were awarded by the jury but no compensatory damages. The CA held that it was perverse and irrational to award exemplary damages but not compensatory.

3. DAMAGES DECIDED BY A JUDGE OR MASTER ALONE
(Damages awarded by judges only have tended to fall within a narrower range)

Case	Facts	Damages
Hayward v Commissioner of Police of the Metropolis (1984) 134 NLJ 724.	An "ordinary respectable Englishman" was wrongfully arrested in the Portobello Road market and was detained for 4½ hours.	Compensatory damages: £1,750 (1996 value: £3,045).
R v Torbay Justices, ex p Pope [1992] CLY 1527, Master Miller.	P was a middle-aged man of good character. He was unlawfully committed to prison for 90 days for non-payment of rates but released on bail after 53 days. He was initially placed in a 2-man cell before being placed with unruly fine defaulters. He was then placed with a double murderer for 21 days which was an uncomfortable experience. He was then placed with a prisoner convicted of the attempted murder of a policeman who was dirty in his habits. He had to "slop out" and was confined to his cell most of the time due to adverse weather conditions.	Compensatory damages: £17,500 (1996 value: £19,600).
Spark v Appraisal Security [1994] CLY 375, Colchester CC.	P was wrongfully detained for 3½ hours as result of an allegation by a store detective.	Compensatory damages of £2,000 for false imprisonment and £500 aggravated damages (1996 value: £2,140 and £535 respectively).

4. AWARDS DECIDED BY A JURY

Case	Facts	Damages
Okot v Comm of Police (1996) Legal Action, 12 February, HHJ Green and a jury, Central London CC.	P falsely imprisoned by 4½ hours to "check immigration status".	Compensatory damages: £2,000.
Leigh-Williams v Chief Constable of Essex (News report, *The Guardian*, 18 October 1990) Michael Davies J and a jury.	P, a former vicar, was unlawfully arrested and detained for 40 hours for breach of the peace. He had previously been lawfully arrested for assault on a 13-year-old boy.	Damages: £4,000 (1996 value: £5,080).
Hajtvassiliou v Commr of Police (1991) Legal Action, 17 January.	P was a Cypriot PhD student who was stopped by the police for speeding and then arrested, assaulted and detained for 2 hours at the police station.	Damages: compensatory £500; aggravated £500; exemplary £4,000 (1996 value: £580, £580, and £4,640 respectively).
Siverne v Chief Constable of Dorset [1994] CLY 249.	P, who had many previous convictions was a guest at a party. Police officers called in response to a claim about the noise and one of them stated he could see a reefer and smell cannabis. There was no written authority to enter the premises and a dispute as to whether permission was given. The occupants were searched but no drugs found. The police alleged that P refused to be searched and that he used threatening and abusive behaviour. P claimed he merely asked to see a search warrant. He was arrested, strip searched at the police station and detained over 7 hours during which time he was denied access to a lavatory. He was convicted of threatening behaviour but successfully appealed.	Following a find that P's behaviour was the result of his resisting an unlawful arrest he was awarded £1,000 for the assault (1996 value: £1,040); £1,500 for false imprisonment (1996 value: £1,560) and £1,750 for malicious prosecution (1996 value: £1,820).

Case	Facts	Damages
Agoba v Chief Constable of Merseyside [1995] CLY Vol 1 1598, Lynch J; Liverpool CC.	P was aged 3 years. His father was arrested and taken to a police station. They were both put in a detention room. P's father was told at 3:30pm that he was to be bailed and then re-arrested on outstanding warrants. P's father then gave full details of P's mother and grandmother and their respective addresses in order for them to be contacted and P taken home. P's family was informed of P's presence at the police station at about 8pm and P was collected at 8:30pm. P was very distressed during his detention and had not been given anything to eat or drink for 3 hours.	Damages: £1,000 was awarded (1996 value: £1,040).
Benjamin v Commr of Police [1995] CLY Vol 1 159; HHJ Quentin Edwards QC; Central London CC.	P was stopped for a motoring offence. Police Officers found a wheelbrace under the driver's seat and as a result of alleged admissions he was arrested. He was falsely imprisoned for 2 hours, charged with possession of an offensive weapon and released. The prosecution was discontinued a few weeks later. P brought an action against the police for false imprisonment, assault and malicious prosecution and claimed that he had never made the admissions that led to his arrest. It was held that he had been falsely imprisoned but not assaulted or maliciously prosecuted.	Damages: compensatory damages: £500 (1996 value: £520). The jury declined to make an award of exemplary damages.
Misra v Commr of Police (1996) Legal Action, 18 January, HHJ Quentin Edwards QC and a jury, Central London CC.	P, who was a university student and of good character, was arrested on information provided by her former flatmates that mail had gone missing from their flat. When arrested she was grabbed firmly by the arm and escorted in full public view to a police van. At the police station she was not allowed to speak to a solicitor of her choice. She was falsely imprisoned from the time of her arrest at 10.55pm for 1 hour 18 minutes.	Compensatory and aggravated damages £1,500 (1996 value: £1,515).
Winyard v Commr of Police (1996) Legal Action, 28 March, Central London CC, HHJ Davis and a jury.	Police officers "planted" a piece of wood on the 23-year-old P, followed him to his flat, assaulted him and detained him. He was arrested and taken to Streatham Police Station, arriving at 12.15am. He was released at 5.05am, just under 5 hours later. He was later acquitted of assaulting the police and carrying an offensive weapon.	Compensatory damages: £14,500. Exemplary damages £50,000.

5. MALICIOUS PROSECUTION

Stark v *Chief Constable of Kent* (News report, *The Guardian*, 14 November 1991) HC.	P was arrested for driving a getaway car during a robbery. He was not told the reason for his arrest and the arresting officer did not have an honest belief in the identification of P.	Compensatory damages: £100 for the assault; £1,000 for malicious prosecution; £15,000. Exemplary damages for the malicious prosecution (1996 value: £116, £1,160 and £17,400 respectively).
Laurence v *Commr of Police*, HL, Popplewell J and a jury (News report, *The Times*, 8 February 1990).	P was knocked to the ground when hit in the face by a police officer's elbow and later maliciously prosecuted for a tax disc offence.	Compensatory damages: £15,000 for malicious prosecution; £50 for the assault. Exemplary damages of £25,000 (1996 value: £19,050, £6,350 and £31,750 respectively).
Marks v *Chief Constable of Greater Manchester*, HC, Hodgson J and a jury (News report, *The Guardian*, 6 December 1991).	P was arrested at the time of a demonstration during Leon Brittan's visit to Manchester. He was maliciously prosecuted for obstructing a police officer in the execution of his duty.	Compensatory damages: £500 for false imprisonment, £5,000 for malicious prosecution. Exemplary damages of £50,000 (1996 value: £580, £5,800 and £58,000 respectively).

Case	Facts	Damages
Gilesnan v Commr of Police (1992, unreported) Westminster CC with a jury.	P was assaulted in the course of a lawful arrest and then maliciously prosecuted for assaulting police officers.	Compensatory damages: £350 for the assault; £15,000 for malicious prosecution. Exemplary damages of £5,000 in respect of the malicious prosecution (1996 value: £390, £16,800 and £5,600 respectively).
Nugent v Commr of Police (News report, *The Guardian*, 15 December 1990).	Police officers fabricated a confession against P who spent one year in prison on remand.	Compensatory damages: £78,456. Exemplary damages £35,750; (1996 value: £99,639 and £45,402 respectively).
Kew v Commr of Police (1994) Legal Action, 16 September, HHJ Rich and a jury; Central London CC.	P was wrongfully arrested and then charged with s 5 of the Public Order Act 1986. In the course of the arrest he sustained slight bruising.	Damages: £50 for assault and battery; £450 for false imprisonment; £12,000 for malicious prosecution (1996 value: £53, £481, £12,840 respectively).
Cannon v Chief Constable of Lincolnshire (3 March 1993, unreported) Lincoln CC with a jury.	Two plaintiffs who had substantial criminal records were assaulted after lawful arrests and then maliciously prosecuted for assaulting police officers. P1 suffered injury to shoulder in the course of the assault.	P1 and P2 received compensatory damages of £250 and exemplary damages of £2,000 for the malicious prosecution. P2 also received £100 for the assault (1996 value: £275, £2,200 and £110 respectively).

Case	Facts	Damages
Spark v *Appraisal Security* [1994] CLY 375, Colchester CC.	P was falsely imprisoned for 3½ hours.	Compensatory and aggravated damages: £2,000 (1996 value: £2,140).
Kownacki v *Commr of Police*, French J and a jury (News report, *The Guardian*, 30 April 1996).	P was a trainee pub manager of good character at the time of his arrest. He was arrested in May 1991 in a well publicised raid on the pub following police surveillance during which police officers allegedly observed P's involvement with drug dealers. He was detained 16 hours and released after being charged with allowing the premises to be used for drug supply and being concerned with the supply of drugs. In Oct 1991 the supply charge was dismissed in an old-style committal. In Dec 1992 the remaining case against P was discontinued. In all, he attended court 6 times. He was unable to get a licence to run his own pub. Evidence was heard that his personality had changed, that he suffered paranoid depression and became bad-tempered.	Damages: compensatory and aggravated damages of £3,000 for false imprisonment and £65,000 for malicious prosecution were awarded. In addition, £40,000 exemplary damages were awarded.
Springer v *British Railways Board* (1996) Legal Action, 28 April, HHJ Wilcox and a jury, Birmingham CC.	P was approached by British Transport Police and asked to leave Birmingham railway station. It was alleged he swore, began to leave, swore again, was cautioned and then assaulted a police officer. The jury found he had not sworn or assaulted the officer, that he had not been warned about his conduct and that he had been forcibly pushed against a bus. He was detained 1½ hours and prosecuted for assaulting a police officer and under s 5 of the Public Order Act 1986. The jury also found the officer had known that he was giving an untrue version of the facts in the civil trial.	Compensatory and aggravated damages £5,250. Exemplary damages £20,000.
Tachie-Menson v *Met Police Commr*, 13 September 1996, unreported, Central London CC, Recorder Goudie QC and a jury.	P was wrongfully arrested after police officers were called to a domestic dispute in which P was involved. He was unlawfully detained thereafter for about 13 hours. He was assaulted during his arrest which resulted in P sustaining permanent laxity of one of the ligaments of his thumb. Following his arrest he was charged with assault occasioning actual bodily harm on a police officer. This was subsequently reduced to assaulting a constable in the execution of his duty. P was acquitted after a full trial.	Damages: compensatory and aggravated damages £10,000 and exemplary damages of £14,000 awarded for false imprisonment, assault and malicious prosecution.

Index

Index

Index